INDIANS IN YELLOWSTONE NATIONAL PARK

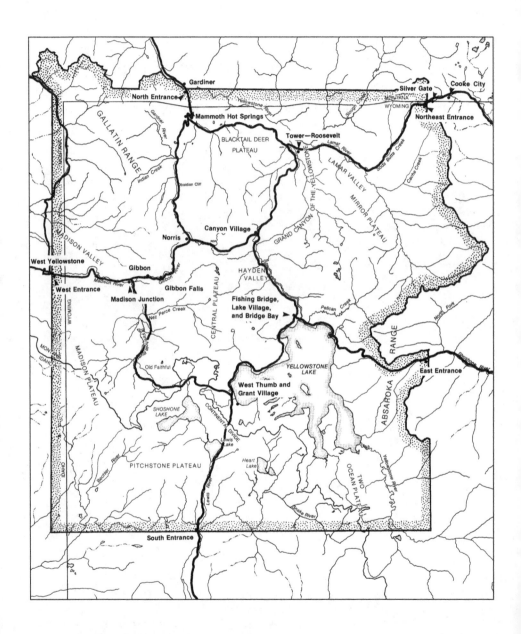

Indians in Yellowstone National Park

Joel C. Janetski

The University of Utah Press

Salt Lake City

Library of Congress Cataloging-in-Publication Data

Janetski, Joel C.

   Indians in Yellowstone National Park / Joel C. Janetski

     p. cm.

Includes bibliographical references.

   ISBN 0-87480-724-7 (pbk. : alk. paper)

   1. Indians of North America—Wyoming. 2. Indians of
North America—Yellowstone National Park. 3. Yellowstone
National Park. I. Title

   E78.W95 J36 2002

   978.7'5200497—dc21

2001008033

Contents

1

The Land

For thousands of years humans have lived in, traveled through, and exploited that vast pine-covered plateau now known as Yellowstone National Park. The millions of visitors pouring through the Park gates today represent an extreme example of this use, but man's presence here is not new. Over the centuries people traveled to Yellowstone for food, clothing, weapons, decorative items, and precious stones, to seek refuge from hostile groups and climates, and to live. Yellowstone is a land of spouting geysers, bubbling mud, boiling springs, and clouds of rising steam and gases—a spectacle that surely astonished indigenous peoples as much as it amazes people today. But it is untrue that native peoples avoided the area in fear of the geysers and hot springs. In fact, man-made objects abound near those thermal features. The deep-rutted trails over which Native Americans crossed the Park to reach the bison-rich plains, remnants of old camps with their conically stacked tipi poles, and extensive log fences for directing game drives can still be seen.

When did people first visit the Park? How long and where did they stay? Did people live here when the first European explorers entered the region? If so, who? And where are those native peoples now? These and other questions are considered below. The answers are based on archaeological research, records and journals of early trappers, explorers, Park officials, and Park records. To understand fully the story of man in Yellowstone, however, it is essential to consider first the natural setting.

The Geologic Record

Yellowstone National Park was and is a region of intense volcanic activity. It consists of a series of high plateaus that average more than 8,000 feet above sea level. These plateaus are composed of extensive flows of welded tuffs, breccias, rhyolite, and basalt, which are 3,000 feet deep near Yellowstone Lake.[1] Below this relatively thin crust lies the Yellowstone Hotspot, a particularly active volcanic region at the northeastern edge of the Yellowstone–Snake River Plain volcanic system. The hotspot, a massive heat source over which the North American Plate moves between 2.5 and 6.5 cm/year,[2] is largely responsible for the Park's geysers, fumaroles, and hot springs. Abundant precipitation feeds these thermal features formed by a combination of geologic events. Three catastrophic, caldera (crater)-forming eruptions in the region produced large, overlapping craters and deposited literally cubic miles of ash-flow tuff.[3] The most recent explosion, about 600,000 years ago in the central area of the Park, spewed ash and lava over much of the Intermountain West and created the 600-square-mile Yellowstone caldera. The magma, or molten rock, just under the caldera surface drained away leaving only a crust, which then collapsed and enhanced the caldera's form. Subsequent lava flows and forest growth have obscured its gigantic size.

The presence of the caldera was not lost on early observer Ferdinand V. Hayden, who in 1871 stood atop Mt. Washburn and noted,

> From the summit of Mt. Washburn, a bird's-eye view of the entire basin may be obtained with the mountains surrounding it on every side without any apparent break in the rim. This basin has been called by some travelers the vast crater of an ancient volcano. It is probable that during the Pliocene period the entire country drained by the sources of the Yellowstone and Columbia was the scene of as great volcanic activity as that of any portion of the globe. It might be called one vast crater, made up of thousands of smaller volcanic vents and fissures out of which the fluid interior of the earth, fragments of rocks and volcanic dust were poured in unlimited quantities.[4]

In addition to volcanic disturbances, the face of Yellowstone was altered by at least three Pleistocene glaciations. Although opinions differ as to times and extent of glaciation, it is generally agreed that the most recent of these, the Pinedale, began about 40,000 years ago and persisted until 12,000 years ago.[5] Evidence suggests that glacial ice up to 1 km thick covered Yellowstone Lake at Pinedale maximum.[6] There is no evidence that people lived in Yellowstone at that time.

The widespread volcanic activity in the Park formed an important raw material that attracted people here early in the human history of North America. When lava cools quickly, volcanic glass, or obsidian, is formed. Obsidian is easily worked and sharpened and was highly valued by Native Americans for cutting tools, projectile points, and, because of its lustrous beauty, decorative items. Before the arrival of Europeans and metal tools, obsidian was traded widely in Mexico, Guatemala, and North America. The best known obsidian source in the Park is Obsidian Cliff, located about halfway between Mammoth Hot Springs and Norris Junction. Yellowstone obsidian varies in color from jet black to "dark to light yellowish brown, purplish brown and olive green."[7] Entertaining and fanciful tales of Obsidian Cliff are attributed to renowned mountain man Jim Bridger, also thought to be one of the first white Americans to see this wonderful geological formation. Early Yellowstone National Park historian Hiram Chittenden recounts Bridger's discovery:

> Coming one day in sight of a magnificent elk, he took careful aim at the unsuspecting animal and fired. To his great amazement, the elk not only was not wounded, but seemed not even to have heard the report of the rifle. Bridger drew considerably nearer and gave the elk the benefit of his most deliberate aim; but with the same result as before. A third and fourth effort met with a similar fate. Utterly exasperated, he seized his rifle by the barrel, resolved to use it as a club since it had failed as a firearm. He rushed madly toward the elk, but suddenly crashed into an immovable vertical wall which proved to be a mountain of perfectly transparent glass, on the farther side of which still in peaceful security, the elk was quietly grazing. Stranger still, the mountain was not only of pure glass, but was a perfect telescopic lens, and whereas the elk seemed but a few hundred yards off, it was in reality twenty-five miles away.[8]

Although the above is a good example of mountain-man exaggeration, Aubrey Haines argued that this story was really about a "glass mountain" in southeast Wyoming, not Obsidian cliff.[9] A version of this story is also found in Stoddard's Lectures, only the animal seen through the "mountain of glass" was a bear.[10]

A highly fanciful account of Native American use of the obsidian is also included here. Imbedded in the following are elements of the myth that Indians were afraid of Yellowstone in the same way children are afraid of the dark and the glib painting of all Indians with a simplistic brush:

> The region of the Yellowstone was to most Indian tribes a place of horror. They trembled at the awful sights they here beheld. But the obsidian cliff was precious to them all. Its substance was as hard as flint, and hence well suited for their arrow-heads. This mountain of volcanic glass was, therefore, the great Indian armory;and as such it was neutral ground. Hither all hostile tribes might come for implements of war and then depart unharmed. While they were here a sacred, intertribal oath protected them. An hour later, those very warriors might meet in deadly combat, and turn against each other's breasts the weapons taken from that laboratory of an unknown power.[11]

Stoddard's characterization of native peoples' fear of the Yellowstone geysers is invalidated by a vast body of empirical data to the contrary (see Chapter 8).

William Henry Holmes, an archaeologist and artist who traveled with the Hayden party in 1872, offered the first scientific description of Obsidian Cliff:

> In ascending Obsidian creek, by way of the newly-cut wagon road which connects Mammoth Hot Springs with the Geyser Basins, we pass first through broad meadows and parked forest. . . . At a point about twelve miles above the junction of the creek with the main stream, there is a narrow gateway known as Obsidian canon. . . . The road approaches the canon along the west side of the valley, and crosses to the east side at the lower end of the canon; in order to avoid the swampy ground that borders the stream it has been carried across the steep debris slopes of the obsidian cliffs. For half a mile it is paved with glassy fragments and lined by huge angular masses of black and banded obsidian rock. From the upper border of the debris slope the vertical cliffs rise to the height of nearly two hundred feet. The lower half is composed of a heavy bed of black obsidian which exhibits some very fine pentagonal columns, somewhat irregularly arranged and frequently distorted, but with perfectly cut faces that glisten

Figure 1. Indians prized obsidian for its lustrous beauty and because it was easily worked. Obsidian Cliff and the surrounding area was an important source of this material. This view of Obsidian Cliff and Beaver Lake was photographed by F. J. Haynes in 1899. [The Haynes Foundation Collection, Montana Historical Society, Helena, Neg. No. H-3940.]

in the sunlight. The upper portion of the wall is composed of a much more obscurely columnar mass of impure spherulitic obsidian, the rude faces of the columns being often as much as ten or twelve feet across.[12]

Holmes became an important figure at the Smithsonian Institution and was well known for his studies of native toolstone quarries.

Obsidian Cliff is enormous, rising 150 to 200 feet above Obsidian Creek and stretching about a half mile, north to south. But obsidian was available to early peoples over a much broader area than Obsidian Cliff. Archaeological work by Les Davis of Montana State University in Bozeman has discovered a wealth of information about the large plateau of which Obsidian Cliffs is but one part.[13] Archaeologists found more than fifty obsidian quarries, visible mostly as pits and trenches, some hundreds of feet long. Despite the presence of many outcrops, tools from only a few found their way into the broader Native American trade network. Other obsidians from the Park were used extensively locally but are not often found outside the Yellowstone and Grand Teton Park areas.[14] More will be said on the obsidian trade in Chapter 2.

Climate and Ecology

Yellowstone climate has not always been what the visitor sees today. At the end of the Pleistocene (about 12,000 years ago), Yellowstone weather was considerably wetter, and up to 5–6°C cooler than it is now. Remnant glaciers clung to the peaks, retreating and advancing as temperatures fluctuated. Studies of ancient pollen indicate that immediately after glacial retreat Yellowstone was largely tundra.[15] Vegetation consisted of a tree-sparse, alpine parkland with sagebrush, grasses, and occasional stands of spruce and bog birch in lower elevations. Megabeasts like mammoth, camel, muskox, and big-horned bison roamed through neighboring Wyoming and likely found their way into the Park, although remains of these animals have not yet been found here.[16] Gradually, the glaciers wasted away, and the cool, wet period was replaced by a drier, warmer climate—the Holocene, the post-Pleistocene geologic epoch. This drying and warming trend began as early as 9,000 years ago and lasted until 4,000 years ago.[17] Plant pollens dated to this period provide evidence for an increase in the fire-adapted species of lodgepole pine, Douglas fir, and quaking aspen. This trend and drier conditions suggest an increase in fires in the Park, and argue for a dynamic forest with stands of various ages and sizes, and greater opportunities for the expansion of grass and sage meadows. Today such meadows also contain blue camas, lilies (both plants with edible roots), and berry bushes.[18] Grasslands, which would have attracted grazing animals, and the presence of food plants suggest an optimum environmental setting for native peoples, who historically used all of these resources. Chapters 2–4 discuss Native American subsistence patterns.

Yellowstone Lake, lying along the eastern edge of the Yellowstone caldera, was at least several feet higher during the late Pleistocene. The Holocene history of Yellowstone Lake levels is complex due to doming of the magma chamber below the caldera and other events characteristic of a geologically dynamic region. Hydrothermal explosions, for example, formed Mary Bay on the lake during the early Holocene. During the Pleistocene-Holocene transition, the beach at Fishing Bridge peninsula would have been similar to that seen at the mouth of nearby Pelican Creek, where a lagoon lies behind a barrier beach north of and slightly higher than the modern beach.[19] For the past 2,000–3,000 years, the climate and environment of Yellowstone have been similar to what we see today.[20] The rich variety of plant and animal life within the Park is due to the wide range of environments.

A bird's-eye view of Yellowstone reveals a country surrounded by substantial mountain ranges. The central and southern portions contain dense lodgepole-pine forests that open gradually into broad parks and sage-grass meadowlands in the Northern Range. Willows grow in abundance along the Madison and Gallatin Rivers on the western border of the Park and south of Yellowstone Lake.[21] Complementing the forests and grasslands are complex river and lake systems with the latter dominated by magnificent Yellowstone Lake, drained by the Yellowstone River. Many of these waterways are fed by water heated by thermal features, often keeping even the slower portions of the rivers ice-free year-round.

Seasonal change is an important characteristic of Yellowstone. Because of the high elevation, winters are long and snow can come any time of year. Snow pack accumulates by November and usually persists until May. Winter temperatures can drop to under –50°F. Snow is commonly four to five feet deep on level ground. Snowdrifts in the high peaks are considerably deeper and linger until July or later. Summers are pleasant and cool, but brief, lasting from mid-June to late August, and are interrupted regularly by showers. Once the high passes are free of snow, traveling is fairly easy, and the Rocky Mountain bighorn sheep move to the high country to avoid the flies so bothersome along the rivers.

Yellowstone waters drain into both the Pacific and Atlantic watersheds. The Bechler and Lewis Rivers channel waters from the Southwest Plateaus into the Snake River Plain and the Pacific drainage. The Madison, Yellowstone, and Clarks Fork Rivers funnel the remainder of the Park's waters to the Missouri and Yellowstone Rivers and eventually to the Gulf of Mexico.

Figure 2. F. Jay Haynes photographed these elk in the snow in Hayden Valley in the winter of 1894. (The Haynes Foundation Collection, Montana Historical Society, Helena, Neg. No. H-3262.)

Animal Resources

Game animals flourish in the Park today and presumably did so in the past. Historic accounts from trappers and early Park travelers as well as archaeological and paleontological research tend to reinforce these conclusions, although populations would have fluctuated with the climates and, perhaps, with human predation. Prehistoric hunters had available elk, mountain sheep, deer, antelope, and bison. Geese, swans, and ducks were common on the fish-filled lakes and rivers. Rabbits, squirrels, marmot, porcupine, beaver, and several species of grouse were common to abundant in season.

Questions about the past abundance of these animals have been difficult to answer.[22] Tantalizing information comes from the priceless journals of early travelers Osborne Russell and William Ferris, both of whom visited the Yellowstone region in the 1830s and recorded their observations.[23] Game seemed especially plentiful near Yellowstone Lake in

Figure 3. Bison in Yellowstone National Park in the late 1800s. Bison were an integral part of Indian life in ancient times. (Photograph by Gifford, Photo Archives, Brigham Young University, Neg. No. P392.)

1836, where Russell reported there were "tall pines forming shady re-treats for the numerous Elk and Deer during the heat of the day." In 1837 he described the Yellowstone Lake country as "swarming with Elk."[24] A contemplative Russell luxuriating in the beauty of Hoodoo Basin notes the "scattered flocks of sheep and elk carelessly feeding."[25]

The evidence for bison in Yellowstone suggests that populations of those animals may have varied over the centuries. Bison bones were found, although not in great quantities, in nearly all lower levels of Lamar Cave, a paleontological site in a sage/grassland setting on the Lamar River, and in several late Holocene archaeological sites in the Park.[26] These finds are conclusive evidence that bison were present in Yellowstone in the past, but just how many is difficult to say. Certainly large herds roamed the grass-rich prairies and the Snake River Plain, but early trapper reports for the Park area seldom mention them. While Os-borne Russell's journal does not mention bison in the Park in the 1830s, he talks about seeing and killing them on the Snake River Plain and on the prairies down the Yellowstone River into Montana. Russell apparently killed a bison "15 miles north" of Jackson's Hole,[27] and William Ferris saw bison there.[28] Miners exploring in the vicinity of Hellroaring Creek in the extreme northern portion of the Park in 1870 encountered "thousands of buffalo quietly grazing" in the area now known as Buffalo Plateau.[29] In the early 1880s Superintendent Norris reported three separate herds spending a portion of the year in the Park: one herd of 200 in the vicinity of Hellroaring and Slough creeks in the north, another of 100 head in the Hoodoo Region to the east, and scattered bands numbering perhaps 300 on the Madison Plateau in the west.[30] He described these bison as "curly, nearly black bison, or mountain buffalo," whose robes he considered "far more valuable than those of the buffalo of the plains."[31] Bison typically wintered outside the Park and were, therefore, fair game for settlers. By the turn of the last century, numbers had dropped to fewer than fifty. The introduction of additional bison from Montana and Texas in the early 1900s and the protection of existing animals brought numbers up steadily, and today more than 3,000 bison roam the Park.[32]

Much of the polemic about game management has focused on elk and bison, the primary large game animals in the Park today. But of interest here are the mountain sheep that once were present in significant numbers and are the namesake for the indigenous peoples who roamed the high country of Idaho and Wyoming. The evidence of substantial populations of mountain sheep comes from early journals, paleontology, and archaeology. Recall, for example, Osborne Russell's description of sheep in Hoodoo Basin. He also documented large concentrations of mountain sheep in the Wind River Mountains that border the Park on the east.[33] John C. Fremont commented on bighorn populations in the Wind River area during the latter half of the nineteenth century.[34] A few decades later Philetus Norris reported that "big-horn sheep are abundant on all the mountain crests, as well as on their craggy spurs and foot-hills throughout the Park, which they never leave."[35] George Frison and his colleagues alluded to "other [historic] reports of large numbers of mountain sheep in the study area [northwestern Wyoming]."[36]

These observations of substantial populations of mountain sheep are reinforced by archaeological findings in Mummy Cave, just east of Yellowstone, where mountain sheep bones were present in every level, even those layers dated to 9000 B.P. (radiocarbon years before present).[37]

Figure 4. Bighorn sheep grazing in Gardner Canyon, 1964. [YNP Photo Archives, No. YELL 27562.]

Lamar Cave, a paleontological site located just east of Tower Junction, offers additional scientific evidence of large game animals in the Park during the distant past. Researchers found bighorn sheep in all but the bottom two levels, documenting bighorn in the Lamar River valley over the past 1,800 years.[38] Perhaps most intriguing, however, are the many drive lines and catch pens still extant in the mountainous country of northwest Wyoming, which are interpreted to be evidence of communal mountain sheep hunting. Some of these are reported in great detail and have been dated to the recent period, which could argue for their construction and use by Sheepeaters.[39] (More will be said about the drive lines themselves in Chapter 4.)

The traps were logically directed at mountain sheep, since the area where they are found is not preferred habitat for other large game. In addition, mountain sheep behavior is broadly predictable and lends to their susceptibility to communal hunting. For example, sheep tend to aggregate in early fall prior to the rut, and it is at this time they would be most available for driving. Frison et al. point out that when disturbed on their bed grounds, bighorn "move rapidly downhill, and then make a half-circle and start uphill."[40] The traps Frison and his colleagues document are placed to intercept the animals once they start uphill. Early park superintendent P. W. Norris observed and described similar drive lines consisting of timber (and occasionally stone) in the Park and also interpreted them as targeting large game.[41] Although Norris does not mention sheep as the intended quarry, many traps were likely constructed for the purpose of hunting them.

It is tantalizing to summarize glibly these diverse data and conclude that elk, or bison, or mountain sheep were (or were not) abundant in the recent or distant past. Any such conclusions should consider the season of observation or kill (in the case of archaeological data) and the region (grasslands, forested region) where the data were gathered. And in a more general sense, the climatic regime for the period must be known since large herbivore populations rise and fall with the availability of forage.[42] That having been said, some modest conclusions seem appropriate regarding the most recent period when Sheepeaters and other historic peoples roamed the Park region. There seems little doubt, for example, that in the early 1800s, elk were common in Yellowstone during the summer months. Russell's comments point to good populations of these large grazers around Yellowstone Lake and the Hoodoo Basin. Mountain sheep were certainly present in substantial numbers, although their range is more restricted than elk, as sheep prefer proximity to rugged country to which they can escape when threatened. The consistent numbers of mountain sheep bones in Lamar Cave, an environment that was largely unchanged for more than 3,000 years, tell us that sheep also frequented grasslands.[43]

The Mummy Cave data and abundant evidence of mountain sheep drive lines argue that mountain sheep were a constant source of food to early peoples. Bison, on the other hand, were apparently present in numbers more modest than today. This is despite current evidence suggesting mesic conditions present on the plains to the east and north.[44]

One could speculate that the rich high-plains grasslands attracted bison away from the mountainous country during this period. Clearly, additional work is needed if the issues raised by numerous scholars are to be resolved.[45]

In addition to these economically useful (to people) species, there were predators. Grizzly and black bear, mountain lion, bobcat, wolf, coyote, fox, and man competed with each other for Yellowstone's resources. Have these predators always been present? Or was the high visibility and presumed high population of animals such as bears simply a function of an artificial food supply? Lamar Cave documents the presence of grizzly bear, wolf, and coyote in the Park for at least the past few thousand years and argues for long-term presence of the animals.[46]

Plant Resources

Descriptions of Yellowstone Park invariably emphasize large game animals and the large predators that prey on them. These highly visible and entertaining species capture the interest and imagination of Park visitors and are the most likely to stop traffic. The casual visitor may view plants as little more than a backdrop for the more animated inhabitants of Yellowstone, and few stop because they have spotted a camas in bloom or a luxuriant stand of chokecherries. Yet Yellowstone's abundant plant life provides habitat and food for all terrestrial—and much aquatic—life and offered critical resources for humans in the past. Wood was used for fuel, housing, and raw material for weapons and a wide spectrum of tools. Plant fibers were used for cordage to make snares, ropes, nets, and clothing. Berries, bulbs, seeds, greens, and nuts diversified and supplemented the diets of the hunters and gatherers who roamed the Park and surrounding areas.

The opening sentence of this chapter referring to Yellowstone as a "vast pine-covered plateau" is simplistic and obscures the great diversity of plants with economic importance to native peoples; however, the phrase is not inaccurate, since more than 75 percent of the Park is covered by dense forest.[47] Forested areas tend to be high in biomass, but the majority of that biomass is in the form of woody trunks and leaves, leaving little for human gatherers. Hayden Valley and the Yellowstone River/Lamar River region in the north and the Bechler Meadows in the southwest offer a lush habitat. Open parklands richly covered with grass and sage, dotted with the occasional stand of conifers, are typical of the Yellowstone/Lamar valleys. These open regions support more biotic diversity than dense forests and were, therefore, more attractive to humans. Accounts of Sheepeater encounters and archaeological sites are most common in or near open spaces or along streams where an array of plants flourished. These, in turn, drew animals, especially grazers and their predators, including people. The Bechler Meadows are best known for stands of camas and sego lily, both gathered for their roots.[48]

Plant communities in all places change with elevation and available moisture, and so it is with Yellowstone.[49] Climatic changes have shifted elevations of those communities over the past 10,000 or so years. Further, a number of the important food plants tend to crosscut vegetation zones.[50] These include a number of root plants such as biscuit root, balsam root, tobacco root, and blue camas.[51] These plants grow in quantity in mid- to lower-elevation meadows and were highly sought as an important nutritional complement by people who relied rather heavily on meat. More will be said about these important foods in later chapters.

Summary

This highly complex, highly diverse system of plants, animals, and humans maintained a natural balance over thousands of years, even while undergoing constant change. Yellowstone Park provided a special setting for peoples, past and present.

2

Precontact History of Yellowstone

Just when man first stood in awe of the geysers and mudpots of Yellowstone we will probably never know, but at least 8,000 to 10,000 years ago American Indians were visiting Yellowstone to hunt and to seek the highly desirable obsidian found there. Archaeological investigations in and near the Park provide rare glimpses of the lifestyle of these earliest visitors. To understand the fragmented story of prehistoric man in Yellowstone, we must assume a continent-wide perspective.

Geological and archaeological research has shown that humans arrived on the North American continent at least 12,000 years ago. It is believed that the primary route by which they drifted into the New World was the broad, 1,300-mile-wide land mass called Beringia. This region, now inundated by the shallow waters of the Bering Sea, was exposed during the late Pleistocene and connected northeastern Asia with Alaska. Although cultural remains from this early period are scattered, archaeological sites in northeastern Canada, Alaska, Pennsylvania, Texas, and elsewhere have been carbon dated from 10,000 to as early as 20,000 B.C.[52]

Archaeological Research in Yellowstone

Much of what is known about Yellowstone's pre-European history comes from archaeological research, beginning with the highly detailed observations by Philetus W. Norris, the second superintendent of the Park. Park historian Aubrey Haines called Norris a "fortunate blend of the pioneer and the scientist."[53] Norris clearly savored exploring, and considered probing research "indispensable for an intelligent and

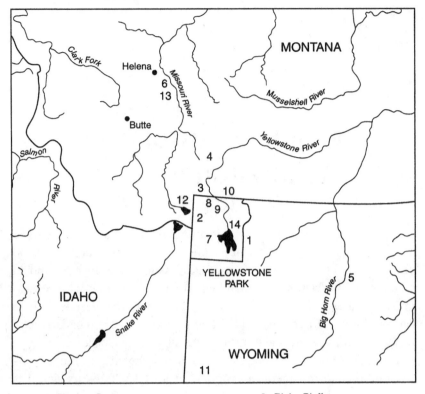

1. Mummy Cave	8. Rigler Bluffs
2. Obsidian Cliffs	9. Blacktail Creek
3. Gardiner Post Office	10. Lookout Mountain sites
4. Anzick Site	11. Wardell Site
5. Colby Site	12. Hebgen Lake
6. McHaffie Site	13. Indian Creek
7. Yellowstone Lake sites	14. Fishing Bridge

Figure 5. Northwest Plains archaeological sites.

judicious performance of the [protection and improvement] of the Park."[54] He collected artifacts, documented archaeological sites, described "Indian" remains that he considered recent evidences of the Sheepeaters, and speculated at some length as to what it all meant. In short, he did what archaeologists do today.

The artifacts Norris collected included several steatite vessel fragments, numerous projectile points, and miscellaneous stone tools. Of particular interest were two "sinkers;" one was "grooved entirely around," and the other exhibited a "hole, 5/8 of an inch from one end."[55] These remarkable objects were discussed at some length in 1896 by Gerard Fowke, who labeled them "plummets" and drew comparisons with the eastern woodlands.[56] Later, Dee Taylor concluded that no comparable artifacts were known from the Intermountain region and argued for connections to the west along the Columbia River to account for them. He also suggested the perforated stone was a decorative item, most likely a pendant. Longitudinally grooved sinkers and well-crafted, perforated stones are known from the Great Basin area as well, although from undated contexts.[57] Norris's failure to mention the origin of the stones—whether he found them in the Park or if they were collected by others—makes conjecture about these intriguing items fruitless.

Important observations were also made by artist and archaeologist W. H. Holmes, who visited Yellowstone with the Hayden Expedition of 1872.[58] Holmes was particularly taken with the obsidian deposits at Obsidian Cliffs. He described them in some detail and speculated on the importance of obsidian to a people who relied on stone for tools:

> It occurred to me, while making examinations at this point, that the various Indian tribes of the neighboring valleys had probably visited this locality for the purpose of procuring material for arrowpoints and other implements. A finer mine could hardly be imagined, for inexhaustible supplies the choicest obsidian, in flakes and fragments of most convenient shapes, cover the surface of the country for miles around.[59]

Holmes knew of obsidian finds in the Midwest and pondered whether it might have been traded to the Hopewell Mounds.[60]

Other important observations were made in the 1940s and 1950s by Park rangers David Condon and Wayne Replogle. Condon served as chief park naturalist from 1946 to 1959, had a penchant for history,[61] and did salvage archaeology on a burial from the Fishing Bridge area in 1941. His description of the find and recovery techniques, which included "screening the contents of the pit dug by the Indians," is remarkably detailed.[62] Replogle also was fascinated by early history and traced the Bannock Trail through the Park.[63]

More systematic research began in the late 1950s when the National Park Service entered into an agreement with Montana State University in Missoula to identify archaeological sites that might be useful in

Figure 6. Mummy Cave with the North Fork of the Shoshone River in the foreground. The cave is located in the center of the photo at the base of the cliff. The two white spots are workers standing in the entrance of the cave. (Buffalo Bill Historical Center, Cody, WY; Jack Richard Collection.)

interpreting the Park's history and to protect known sites from potentially destructive development. Directed by Carling Malouf and Dee Taylor, crews completed two seasons of work in 1958 and 1959 and documented 224 sites in the Park.[64] They also tested the First Blood Site on Yellowstone Lake, so named because it was the first place pottery was found.[65] This first professional work formed a foundation of reliable information about Yellowstone prehistory.

Without a doubt the most important archaeological site in the region is Mummy Cave. The discovery and excavation of this site proved to be a milestone in understanding the great depth of regional human history. The work was overseen by Harold McCracken, then director of the Buffalo Bill Historical Center and Whitney Gallery in Cody, Wyoming, who began a formal search for promising archaeological sites in 1962.[66]

Figure 7. Ongoing excavations at Mummy Cave, about 1964. Project director Harold McCracken stands third from the left. (Buffalo Bill Historical Center, Cody, WY; Jack Richard Collection.)

Waldo Wedel of the Smithsonian encouraged McCracken to look for caves in which early human remains might be found. Soon after, Robert Edgar, an amateur archaeologist and field assistant, took McCracken to the cave, where they quickly recognized its potential. The project was underway. None anticipated the great depth of cave deposits (33-plus feet) that eventually yielded 38 separate layers of cultural debris documenting 9,000 years of human use. McCracken later hired Wilfred Husted to take over the excavations. The materials recovered from the cave were reported in 1978, and reanalysis of the collections continues.[67]

Although the above work made important contributions, Yellowstone Park itself was not well known. In 1982, archaeologist Gary Wright referred to Yellowstone as "one of the poorest known archeological areas of North America."[68] He and his colleagues and students Susan Bender, Thomas Marceau, Stuart Reeve, Rosemary Smith, Anne Samuelson, and others did much to change that with their work in Jackson Hole and Grand Teton and Yellowstone National Parks.[69]

During the 1990s Leslie B. Davis and students and colleagues from Montana State University and the National Park Service brought wonderful insights into the importance and extent of Yellowstone obsidian use during the precontact period.[70] Researchers from the Museum of the Rockies at Montana State University surveyed the length of the Yellowstone River in the Park and tested several sites.[71] National Park Service archaeologist Kenneth P. Cannon has been active in Yellowstone archaeology. His many publications include a multidisciplinary project at Fishing Bridge,[72] ecological research revolving around bison, and, with Richard Hughes, additional research on obsidian use.[73] Research by archaeologists from the Museum of the Rockies added significant details to pre-European lifeways in Yellowstone.[74] The work of these scholars makes the following synthesis of Yellowstone precontact history possible.

Paleoindians (10,000–6000 B.C.)

Archaeological investigations at many locales in North America have demonstrated that by 9000 B.C. a distinctive lifeway had developed on the High Plains from Alberta to Texas.[75] This early culture, called the Paleoindian or Big Game Hunting period, is characterized by the pursuit of large, now-extinct mammals such as mammoth, long-horned bison, and the horse, although smaller animals and plant foods were undoubtedly part of the diet as well. These animals were killed with spears or darts tipped with distinctive stone projectile points thrown by an atlatl, or spear-throwing stick. The Great Basin and Columbia Plateau, both adjacent to Yellowstone, were also occupied earlier than 10,000 years ago, although the lifestyle there appears to have been less focused on hunting.[76]

The earliest, well-defined Paleoindian culture has been labeled Clovis, after the town in eastern New Mexico near where it was first identified.[77] From 9500 to 9000 B.C., Clovis hunters pursued proboscideans such as mammoth (*Mammuthus columbi*) and mastodon (*Mammut americanum*), horse, bison, and an array of smaller animals. Mammoth remains together with the easily recognizable lanceolate, half-fluted, projectile points and finely crafted blades are generally recognized as the calling cards of Clovis hunters.[78]

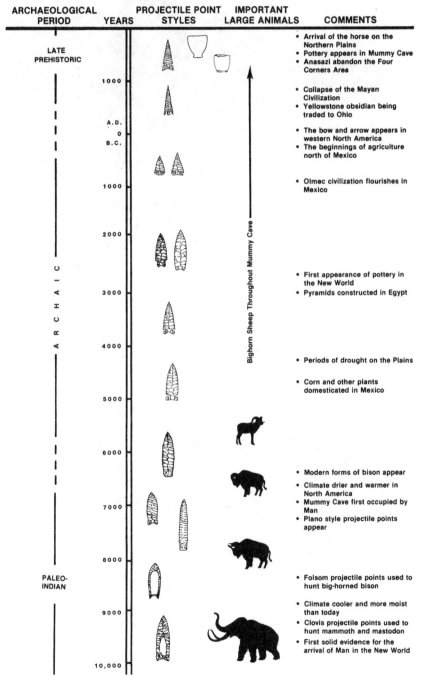

CHRONOLOGY
OF THE
NORTHERN INTERMOUNTAIN REGION

ARCHAEOLOGICAL PERIOD	YEARS	PROJECTILE POINT STYLES	IMPORTANT LARGE ANIMALS	COMMENTS
LATE PREHISTORIC				• Arrival of the horse on the Northern Plains • Pottery appears in Mummy Cave • Anasazi abandon the Four Corners Area
	1000			• Collapse of the Mayan Civilization • Yellowstone obsidian being traded to Ohio
	A.D. 0 B.C.			• The bow and arrow appears in western North America • The beginnings of agriculture north of Mexico
	1000			• Olmec civilization flourishes in Mexico
	2000			
ARCHAIC	3000			• First appearance of pottery in the New World • Pyramids constructed in Egypt
	4000			• Periods of drought on the Plains
	5000			• Corn and other plants domesticated in Mexico
	6000			
	7000			• Modern forms of bison appear • Climate drier and warmer in North America • Mummy Cave first occupied by Man • Plano style projectile points appear
	8000			• Folsom projectile points used to hunt big-horned bison
PALEO-INDIAN	9000			• Climate cooler and more moist than today • Clovis projectile points used to hunt mammoth and mastodon • First solid evidence for the arrival of Man in the New World
	10,000			

Bighorn Sheep Throughout Mummy Cave

Figure 8. (Opposite) Chronology of the Northern Intermountain region based on Mummy Cave excavations and other archaeological findings.

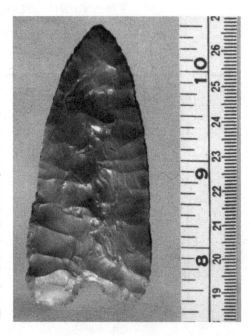

Figure 9. A projectile point resembling Clovis points from the Colby Site in Wyoming and in the Fenn Cache, as reported by George C. Frison and Bruce Bradley, *The Fenn Cache, Clovis Weapons and Tools* [Santa Fe: One Horse Land and Cattle Company, 1999]. This artifact was found in 1953 by James L. Whitlock at the mouth of Sheffield Creek two miles south of the south gate of Yellowstone National Park. [Courtesy of Forrest Fenn collection.]

Several centuries after the appearance of Clovis, a change occurred. Perhaps due to climatic conditions and overhunting, mammoth became scarce. Big Game Hunters sought long-horned bison (*Bison antiquus*), using Folsom points. These unique, superbly crafted stone tools had long, wide flake scars (flutes) that were removed from the base of the point and extended to the distal or pointed end of both faces of the tool. Folsom points were smaller than and made differently from Clovis points. The latter were largely finished by a flaking technique called percussion, which involved striking the point with light blows with a bone, wood, or antler baton to remove stone flakes to shape the point. Folsom points were finished by pressure flaking, accomplished by placing the point of the flaking tool exactly where the flake was to be removed and pressing down. Folsom points were also first identified in New Mexico but were widespread across western North America. Fluted points, especially Clovis, have also been found throughout the Midwest and eastern North America. Their makers preferred high-quality tool stone and obtained materials over great distances.[79] Both of these projectiles were used to tip wooden shafts thrown either as spears or, more likely, with atlatls.

The Folsom period spanned about 1,000 years, from 9000 to 8000 B.C., after which fluted points went out of style. But hunting large game, especially a smaller form of ancient bison, *Bison occidentalis,* continued. This period, the Late Paleoindian, is characterized by the use of a variety of large, lanceolate projectile points all produced using a highly sophisticated pressure flaking technology. These points are variously called Agate Basin, Hell Gap, Eden, Scottsbluff, Alberta, or Angostura, depending on slight differences in size, shape, and the geographical area where they were first identified. Ages vary and, in some cases, overlap with the Folsom period. At the end of this era, about 6000 B.C., Big Game Hunting gave way to a more generalized subsistence pattern. Before describing this major change, let's examine evidence of the Big Game Hunting period in Yellowstone.

Paleoindian Period in Yellowstone

Man apparently visited the Yellowstone area in the Paleoindian period. In 1959 the base of an obsidian Clovis point was uncovered during the construction of the post office building at Gardiner, Montana. It is not known if the material is from Yellowstone sources.[80] Additional evidence of Clovis near the Park comes from the Anzick Site at Wilsall, Montana, a short distance north of Gardiner. Here archaeologists found a rare Clovis burial with finely made bone projectile points and massive, finished and unfinished Clovis-like stone points.[81] Unusual Clovis points and mammoth remains were found at the Colby site in the Big Horn Basin of Wyoming.[82] To date, no Clovis points have been found within Yellowstone.

Nor have any Folsom-age remains been found inside the Park. However, Paleoindian visits to Yellowstone are documented by an obsidian Folsom point found just south of the Park in the Bridger-Teton National Forest. The obsidian has been chemically traced to the Obsidian Cliffs area.[83] Folsom occupations have also been found in buried deposits at the McHaffie and Indian Creek sites just south of Helena, Montana,[84] and on the surface in southwest Montana. Owl Cave on Idaho's Snake River Plain contained Folsom material and evidence of bison hunting.[85]

In contrast to the Clovis and Folsom periods, the Late Paleoindian period is well represented in the Park. Archaeological surveys by University of Montana archaeologists in the late 1950s found several late

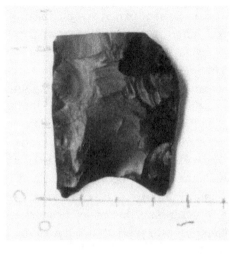

Figure 10. Clovis projectile point base from Gardiner, Montana. (Aubrey Haines, photographer, YNP Photo Archives, Neg. No. YELL 37031.)

Paleoindian artifacts, including Agate Basin and Hell Gap projectile points and a distinctive tool called a Cody knife. The latter is characteristic of the Cody Complex, a Late Paleoindian culture.[86] A number of Late Paleoindian points, including the large lanceolate Agate Basin, Hell Gap, and Eden styles, are recorded from the Lookout Mountain region north of the Park. Of particular interest is that the points were found on ridges over 9,000 feet in elevation, demonstrating that early hunters did not restrict their travels to the lower plains where their presumed primary quarry, the bison, was found.

Until recently, Late Paleoindian tools had been recovered only from the ground surface and constituted circumstantial evidence of occupation. Buried deposits dated by radiocarbon analysis or other means are needed to substantiate the presence of an ancient people in an area at any given time. The dates assumed for surface points are based on typological cross-dating. That is, even though a particular find has not been directly dated, other sites with typologically similar materials have been, and those dates can be assumed with a degree of confidence for artifacts such as those found in Yellowstone. Mummy Cave, for instance, was occupied sporadically over a 9,000-year period.[87] It has been excavated and the various strata dated. Arrow and atlatl dart points from dated levels can be cross-dated to surface finds in the vicinity. The cornerstone of archaeological dating is stratigraphy, or superposition. Simply stated, superposition assumes that the materials on the bottom in any undisturbed site were laid down first and are, therefore, the oldest.

Recent research by Park Service archaeologists near Fishing Bridge found Late Paleoindian–style projectile points on the surface and in the subsurface excavations.[88] Also, archaeologists excavating a large site on Jackson Lake in Grand Teton National Park found a number of Cody knives.[89] In addition to these Late Paleoindian finds, which suggest connections or at least similarities to Plains groups at that time, a Haskett point of Obsidian Cliff obsidian was discovered on Grayling Creek near the west boundary of the Park.[90] These spear or dart points date to approximately the same period as the Cody material, but are generally found in Washington, Oregon, and Idaho, and represent interaction in some form with these areas. These findings are evidence that, because of its geographic location, Yellowstone received human visitors and influences from both the east and the west.

Many of the Late Paleoindian points mentioned here are made of obsidian and some were clearly quarried in Yellowstone. Researchers have found that these early hunters tended to use a greater variety of obsidian sources than later peoples did. Late Paleoindian points found in the Park were made of obsidian quarried in southern and eastern Idaho and at Obsidian Cliff.[91]

The archaeological evidence shows that Big Game Hunters came to Yellowstone more than 7,500 years ago, presumably to hunt but certainly to quarry obsidian.

Archaic (6000 B.C.–A.D. 1)

With the gradual change from the cooler and wetter early post-Pleistocene to the warmer and drier climate we know today, giant bison, mammoth, horse, camel, and other large mammals became extinct. The human lifeway that depended largely on them was replaced by a broader economic pattern of exploitation—the Archaic period. It is characterized by a greater reliance on plant foods, especially small seeds, and the increased hunting of smaller animals, although the modern large animals—deer, mountain sheep, and bison—continued to be important.

These resources were hunted and gathered during a carefully scheduled yearly round, a system that took shape over hundreds, even thousands of years. The yearly round was based on the season of the year when particular plants and animals were best gathered or hunted. Fish were sought when they were concentrated in their spawning runs, seeds when they were ripe in the greatest numbers, rabbits when they were the fattest. As a result, the movements of the people assumed a definite, predictable pattern based on timely utilization of available resources. Their standard tools were baskets for gathering seeds and nuts, stone grinding implements to process them, and the atlatl and snares for hunting.

Archaic Period in Yellowstone

The Archaic period is well documented in Yellowstone. The reason for man's increased presence may, in large part, be climatic. Some have suggested that the High Plains suffered increased aridity after about 7000 B.C. and were not the favorable areas for habitation they had been during the Big Game Hunting period.[92] Although this has not been clearly demonstrated, it is the case that higher elevations such as the Black Hills and the Rocky Mountains, including Yellowstone, were increasingly visited by humans, perhaps due to more dependable food and water supplies. In Yellowstone, Archaic sites are recognized by the presence of large, side-notched projectile points. These artifacts first appear about 7,000 years ago in Archaic levels of dated sites such as Mummy Cave. The Yellowstone River valley from the mouth of the Gardner River down to Yankee Jim Canyon contains a number of sites believed to have been used as winter camps during this period. The Rigler Bluffs site near Corwin Springs contained an ancient fire hearth dated to about 5,000 years ago.[93] Wood recovered from the hearth was identified as western yew, a moisture-loving tree not now found in the area. This hints that several thousand years ago the Yellowstone River Valley may have received more precipitation than it does now. The presence of the yew wood was explained in part by geological studies of the Rigler Bluff Site. The hearth was located well away from and above the river, a fact that at first puzzled the scientists. Sediment analysis above and below the hearth concluded that about 5,000 years ago the Yellowstone River had been blocked by a massive landslide, not unlike that which dammed up the Madison in 1959 and formed a lake. The hearth was situated along the edge of that lake.

The earliest absolute dates associated with cultural material in the Park come from the Chittendon Bridge site east of Mammoth Hot Springs on the Gardner River. Age estimates from obsidian hydration dating place the earliest use of this site at about 7,000 years ago.[94] The excavators argue that in the absence of bones from large game, and given the kinds of stone tools found (mostly small flakes and blades), this site was used for fishing. However, no fish bones are mentioned, and site function is best considered inconclusive. Archaic occupations that include rock-fired features have also been found at the mouth of Arnica Creek on Yellowstone Lake and date to about 4500 B.P. These features contained evidence of non-economic, water-loving plants but could have been used for roasting roots. Additional concentrations of Archaic sites are reported on the West Gallatin River, in the Clark Fork River valley, the north fork of the Shoshone River, and the Corey Springs area on the northeast shore of present Hebgen Lake.

Research at the massive Lawrence Site in Grand Teton National Park provides additional insights into native life in the Park. Evidence points to the importance of root crops, especially blue camas, perhaps beginning as early as the mid-Archaic period and continuing into the Late Prehistoric era (see below).[95] Blue camas belongs to a larger vegetational community that includes biscuit root, arrow leaf balsam root, and mules ears, all of which were used as food by native peoples. That community has been documented in Yellowstone as well.[96] Camas was important to native peoples wherever it occurred (see Chapter 7).

Archaeological support from the Lawrence Site for the importance of this suite of root crops includes the presence of roasting facilities evidenced by numerous concentrations of fire-cracked rock, the tendency for archaeological sites in the area to occur near modern stands of blue camas, and abundant grinding stones (including mortars and pestles), presumably for pounding roots either for immediate consumption or preparatory to making them into cakes for long-term storage.[97] It should also be noted that amateurs have collected an estimated 1,000 projectile points from the area. This tells us that hunting was also an important subsistence activity. It is possible that this locale on scenic Jackson Lake was the setting for a late spring to early summer annual gathering of peoples from the region.[98]

Late Prehistoric (A.D. 1–1500)

The Archaic lifestyle persisted in some parts of North America until the time of European contact. However, shortly after the time of Christ, changes occurred that affected the eastern Great Basin and Colorado Plateau and, to a certain extent, Yellowstone. These changes marked the end of the Archaic and the beginning of a more settled life in much of North America. Included are the adoption of horticulture, or the planting of crops, the use of the bow and arrow and ceramic vessels, and the construction of more substantial houses. In the American Southwest and eastern United States, horticulture spurred increasing sedentism (settled lifestyles), population growth, village life, and a more complex societal organization. During this period the Anasazi constructed great houses in New Mexico's Chaco Canyon and the Hohokam built massive canal systems around present-day Phoenix. East of the Mississippi River a complex religion not well understood by scholars resulted in the construction of a large number of burial mounds between 500 B.C. and A.D. 800. Filled with bones and grave offerings, many mounds were of great size and built in the shape of animals and geometric forms. The mounds are now assigned to the Adena/Hopewell period. They were a source of amazement and entertainment for eighteenth- and nineteenth-century antiquarians who dug for relics and destroyed many of the mounds before research-oriented archaeology was attempted.[99]

Among the many grave goods recovered were items foreign to the region. These exotic items included conch shells from the Gulf of Mexico, elaborately carved pieces of mica from the southeastern United States, grizzly bear claws from the western plains, and obsidian tools (including flakes and blades, large spears, knives, eccentrics, and projectile points), long suspected to be from either Yellowstone or Mexico (see discussion below).

Late Prehistoric in Yellowstone

Although agriculture was never important in Yellowstone or neighboring areas, the agricultural societies that flourished to the east were connected to the Rocky Mountains and Yellowstone obsidian through trade or direct visitation. William Henry Holmes's comments on this topic are illustrative:

With respect to the origin of the great numbers of obsidian implements found in the Hopewell mounds, it may be well to note
there is no trace of Mexican characters in the pottery of these
mounds; besides, the general trend of the group of wares [pot-
tery] here associated is from Chillicothe towards the northwest,
suggesting the upper Missouri region or the valley of the Columbia as the source of the Obsidian. The significance of this observation is emphasized by the discovery of fragments of rouletted
ware in the Yellowstone National Park, where great beds of obsidian are found.[100]

To resolve these questions scientists analyzed obsidian artifacts from
thirty sites in Ohio, Illinois, Indiana, Michigan, and Ontario and successfully demonstrated that the obsidian used by these Hopewellian
peoples was quarried more than 1,500 miles away at Obsidian Cliffs and
one other source in the Park.[101] It is not known if the obsidian was obtained by Hopewell traders who traveled to Yellowstone in person, or if
it was traded from hand to hand until it finally reached the Hopewell.
Archaeological research between the Park and the Midwest has identified Yellowstone obsidian in Iowa, North Dakota, and Oklahoma.[102]
These findings suggest that it is more likely that obsidian was traded
from village to village until it finally reached the Hopewell region. The
Yellowstone-Missouri-Mississippi river system may have been a route
for this transport.

Yellowstone obsidian spread in directions other than east during the
Late Prehistoric period. This toolstone has now been documented in
Washington, Alberta, Saskatchewan, Colorado,[103] and central Utah,
where it appears after 1300.[104] In general, Yellowstone obsidian seems to
increase in use through time and is more commonly used on the Northwestern plains than in the Intermountain area and Great Basin, where
Idaho and Oregon obsidians are more common.[105]

Although agriculture was not important to the Plains and Great Basin
Indians who traveled through the Park, hunting was. The transition
from the atlatl to the more accurate, more powerful, and more easily ma-
nipulated bow and arrow is marked archaeologically by the appearance
of smaller, finer projectile points—arrowheads. In dry sites like Mummy
Cave the change is also visible through the appearance of bow and arrow
fragments.

Figure 11. Blades of Yellowstone obsidian from Hopewell mounds in Ohio. (Field Museum of Natural History, W. K. Moorehead 1922, Neg. Nos. 31233 and 31235.)

Cooperative hunting of large herds of bison had a tradition dating to late Folsom times, but communal drives became more common on the northwestern plains during the Late Prehistoric period. The earliest known bison drive in the area in which the bow and arrow was used is the Wardell Site near Big Piney, Wyoming, dated to about 500.[106] This site also contains another new and important item of material culture—pottery. Pottery is useful to archaeologists because it preserves well and can be used as an excellent time-marker since it is sensitive to nuances in change of form, construction, and decoration. The pottery at Wardell consisted of shards from plainware jars with pointed bottoms, a style unlike the flat-bottomed Intermountain pottery that appears perhaps as much as 1,000 years later. Intermountain pottery vessels were usually wide-mouthed jars with a flat, flanged base. Pottery appears quite late in Yellowstone. In the 30 feet of deposits at Mummy Cave, only the top 15 or 20 inches contain pottery.

The first site in the Park to yield controlled evidence of pottery was the First Blood Site near the mouth of Arnica Creek near West Thumb Bay on Yellowstone Lake, which yielded Intermoutain pottery from

Figure 12. Intermountain pottery from southern Wyoming. (George C. Frison, *Prehistoric Hunters of the High Plains*, Academic Press.)

buried deposits.[107] Norris reported ceramics associated with a fragment of a steatite vessel eroding out of the bank on Blacktail Creek.[108] These stone pots are nearly identical in form to the flat-bottomed ceramic pots, but are smaller and made of the soft stone, steatite. Several are reported from the Park,[109] including four fragmented stone vessels that Norris found, but none are dated and their makers are not clearly identified. Steatite sources are known in the Big Horn, Wind River, and Teton Mountains of Wyoming, and steatite in various forms (pipes, beads, plates, and bowls) is found widely scattered in the region around Yellowstone.[110] Pottery was also recently discovered at the Ryder Site, a multicomponent occupation in the Black Canyon of the Yellowstone River.[111]

The Late Prehistoric period in Yellowstone is a time of heavy occupation. The first archaeological site recorded in the Park is located near Fishing Bridge and most likely dates to the Late Prehistoric period.[112] The site is a burial uncovered in 1941 by a workman digging a sewer

Figure 13. Carved steatite vessel from Wyoming. (George C. Frison, *Prehistoric Hunters of the High Plains*, Academic Press.)

trench. David Condon, the park naturalist mentioned earlier, heard of the find and was able to preserve some information about it. An adult male, several "arrowheads" and other chipped stone tools, a pestle, an elk antler tool, and two dogs were buried in an oval pit. The grave was filled and then covered with numerous round stones. If the projectile points are identified correctly as arrowheads, they argue that the site dates after A.D. 200, the approximate time when bows and arrows became widespread on the Northern Plains and in the Great Basin.[113] The drawings in Condon's article are crude, making clear determination of whether the tools are arrow or atlatl points difficult. Fortunately, Dee Taylor includes photos of two of these points in his report and describes them in detail sufficient to conclude they are arrowheads. Recent analysis identifies one as similar to Avonlea, an early arrow point on the Northern Plains,[114] a strong argument for a Late Prehistoric date for this burial.

Figure 14. Artifacts found by Supt. P. W. Norris, presumably in Yellowstone: a) portion of a steatite bowl and b) stone "sinker." (YNP Photo Archives, Neg. No. YELL 37033-2.)

a   b

In 1956 another burial was discovered by a backhoe operator digging a water line in the Fishing Bridge campground area. A dog was also found in this grave, but the age of the interment is not clear.[115]

The Yellowstone River Valley at the north end of the Park is littered with sites from this era. Recent archaeological excavation of a 1,500-year-old hearth along the river found evidence of fish, elk, bighorn sheep, and prickly pear cactus. The archaeological and paleontological record from Yellowstone now argues for a possible increase in the numbers of (or human use of) elk at this time.[116] Isolated summer camps dating to the Late Prehistoric are found throughout the Plateau Region. Wickiups, stone blinds, and log alignments for hunting bighorn sheep and other large game are primarily relics of this period, which immediately precedes the arrival of Europeans. Philetus Norris assigned these remains to the Sheepeaters, a Shoshone group that traveled through the

Figure 15. Bison bone bed exposed by archaeological excavation on the north shore of Yellowstone Lake. (Photo courtesy of Kenneth Cannon, National Park Service.)

mountainous country of Idaho and northwestern Wyoming. (See Chapters 3 and 4 for more on the historic Native Americans.) In reality, it is difficult to say for certain that these drive lines or other visible remnants of human presence belonged to Sheepeaters.

Summary

This overview of archaeological evidence of people in Yellowstone is a quick sketch of a rich and complex past. Given the long time spans involved, data are relatively few, but research continues. New findings will undoubtedly require revisiting this history. The Native American's post-contact use of Yellowstone, documented by observation, is richer still and presented in the following chapter.

3

Historic Native Americans in Yellowstone

Understanding aboriginal use of Yellowstone in the recent past requires a broader perspective than just the Park, as events occurring even at great distances eventually had an impact on the lives of those living in the Intermountain region.[117] The arrival of European explorers in the fifteenth century, and later settlers, technology, diseases, and social, political, and religious systems mark the Historic period in North America. All of these were new to the Indians of America, and the changes brought to ancient lifeways were profound and, almost without exception, disastrous.

The use of the horse completely altered the lifestyle of many Indians of the Intermountain West. Before 1600, several Plains groups—Sioux, Cheyenne, Crow, and others—were farmers living in villages well to the east of their later locations. The horse changed all of that, as it provided a new means of transportation and more efficient methods of hunting bison.

The Spanish brought horses in considerable numbers to their settlements in Texas and New Mexico. From there the horse spread to the plains and plateaus of western North America, reaching the Shoshone living on the plains of Wyoming and eastern Idaho by 1700–1720.[118] As long as they had grasslands to fuel their transportation, mounted groups were able to move quickly over long distances while pursuing the bison or enemies. They could now take their families, carry more baggage, and live in greater comfort. Many Intermountain and Plains tribes adopted the horse and developed a nomadic lifestyle (characterized by tipis, the pursuit of bison, and warrior societies), which combined to

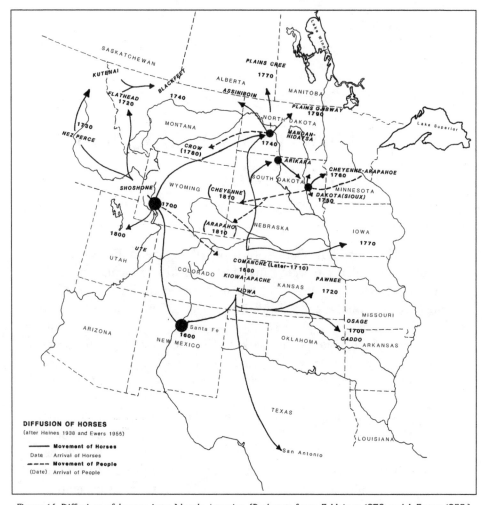

Figure 16. Diffusion of horses into North America. (Redrawn from F. Haines 1938 and J. Ewers 1955.)

constitute the classic Plains Culture glamorized in western movies and fictional literature.

Those who obtained horses first had a distinct advantage. For example, the Shoshone of the northeastern Great Basin and southwestern Wyoming obtained horses by 1720, about 10 to 20 years before their traditional foes the Blackfeet. Mounted, and armed with iron trade weapons, the Shoshone expanded as far north as Saskatchewan, pushing their enemies ahead of them. This success was short lived, however. The Blackfeet, armed with guns from British and French traders, forced the Shoshone back into Wyoming and Idaho by the last quarter of the eighteenth century.[119]

Nearly all of the tribes in the Yellowstone region eventually adopted the horse, including groups who lived primarily west of the continental divide—the Flathead, Nez Perce, Kalispel, Coeur d'Alene, and the Shoshone-Bannock. Many made annual treks to the Montana and Wyoming prairies to hunt bison on horseback. The Blackfeet, Crow, and Eastern or Wind River Shoshone were Yellowstone-area tribes who lived on the Plains, adopted the horse, and became part of the Plains culture. Groups from both sides of the divide commonly traveled through or camped in the area now known as Yellowstone. Those most frequently mentioned are the Blackfeet, Crow, and Shoshone-Bannock.

At the time of Lewis and Clark's expedition up the Missouri, the Blackfeet controlled the region north of the Park, although they occasionally ranged as far south as Idaho and northern Utah. The Crow lived northeast and east along and south of the Yellowstone River, while various Shoshone-speakers[120] occupied the country west, south, and southeast of Yellowstone. In the upper Snake River Valley were the Bannock, an enclave of Northern Paiute people who lived side-by-side with their linguistic cousins the Shoshone. Living within Yellowstone Park and the adjacent mountains were groups of Shoshone-speakers who were called the Sheepeaters because the bighorn sheep was an important game animal to them. The Sheepeaters were the primary occupants of Yellowstone during the Historic period (see Chapter 4).

The boundaries separating these groups were certainly not absolute, and all crossed or stayed in the Park at various times. The Wind River Shoshone—also called Washakie's Band after their legendary leader, whose life spanned much of the recent Historic period—and the Eastern Shoshone often spent summers in the vicinity of Yellowstone, where they quarried steatite and obsidian and camped and fished around Yellowstone Lake. They also used the waters of the hot springs and pools for religious and medicinal purposes. Although the Sheepeaters apparently spent more time in the Park than other groups did, it is important to discuss the Blackfeet and Crow and provide some background on the Shoshone-Bannock, to whom the Sheepeaters were closely related.

Blackfeet

The Blackfeet Indians speak Algonkian, a language related to those of a number of tribes of central and eastern Canada. The linguistic relationships are relatively distant and suggest a fairly early separation from other Algonkian speakers. Unlike the Cheyenne, Crow, and some other Plains groups, the Blackfeet lived on the Northwestern plains for a considerable time before the advent of the horse.[121] The Blackfeet were further divided into three loosely affiliated, interacting groups: the Pikuni or Piegan, the Kainah or Blood, and the Blackfeet. The term "Blackfeet" is a fairly literal translation of the Algonkian name *Siksikauw* (black-footed people).[122]

The Blackfeet were notorious for their warlike attitude, and during the 1700s and 1800s were the undisputed rulers of the plains of central Montana and southern Alberta. Blackfeet historian John Ewers describes this tribe as the most feared of all tribes in the West.[123] Intertribal conflict was not systematic or aimed at killing individuals, but focused on personal glory and gain in the form of courageous exploits or stealing horses. Ambitious young men were the most likely to take chances, and successful warriors credited their powerful war medicine rather than personal prowess.[124] Raiding parties consisting of small groups carrying minimum gear mounted on their war ponies roamed widely in search of opportunity to achieve special status. Such travels took Blackfeet warriors as far south as northern Utah and occasionally through Yellowstone.

The presence of the Blackfeet in Yellowstone is heavily documented in the journals of early trappers like Jim Bridger, Daniel Potts, W. A. Ferris, and Osborne Russell. Russell tells of a number of encounters with Blackfeet in Jackson Hole, on the Madison River near present-day Ennis, Montana, and inside the Park on Pelican Creek on the north side of Yellowstone Lake. Russell describes such an event in August 1839 (spelling and punctuation are his):

> We were encamped about a half a mile from the Lake on a
> stream running into it in a S.W. direction thro. a prarie bottom
> about a quarter of a mile wide On each side of this valley arose a
> bench of land about 20 ft high running parallel with the stream
> and covered with pines On this bench we were encamped on the
> SE side of the stream The pines immediately behind us was

Figure 17. Double Steel and Two Cutter, Blackfeet Indian women portrayed by artist Winhold Reiss on a Great Northern Railroad calendar.

thickly intermingled with logs and fallen trees—After eating a few [minutes] I arose and kindled a fire filled my tobacco pipe and sat down to smoke My comrade whose name was White was still sleeping. Presently I cast my eyes towards the horses which were feeding in the Valley and discovered the heads of some Indians who were gliding round under the bench within 30 steps of me I jumped to my rifle and aroused White and looking towards my powder horn and bullet pouch it was already in the hands of an Indian and we were completely surrounded We cocked our rifles and started thro. their ranks into the woods which seemed to be completely filled with Blackfeet who rent the air with their horrid yells. on presenting our rifles they opened a space about 20 ft. wide thro. which we plunged about the fourth jump an arrow struck White on the right hip joint I hastily told him to pull it out and as I spoke another arrow struck me in the same place but they did not retard our progress At length another arrow striking thro. my right leg above the knee benumbed the flesh so that I fell with my breast across a log. The Indian who shot me was within 8 ft and made a Spring towards me with his uplifted battle axe: I made a leap and avoided the blow and kept hopping from log to log thro. a shower of arrows which flew around us like hail, lodging in the pines and logs. After we had passed them about 10 paces we wheeled about and took [aim] at them They then began to dodge behind the trees and shoot their guns we then ran and hopped about 50 yards further in the logs and bushes and made a stand—I was very faint from the loss of blood and we set down among the logs determined to kill the two foremost when they came up and then die like men we rested our rifles across a log White aiming at the foremost and Myself at the second I whispered to him that when they turned their eyes toward us to pull trigger. About 20 of them passed by us within 15 feet without casting a glance towards us another file came round on the [opposite] side with 20 or 30 paces closing with the first a few rods beyond us and all turning to the right the next minute were out of our sight among the bushes They were all well armed with fusees, bows & battle axes.[125]

Russell and his companion were not discovered, and, after enduring considerable pain from their wounds and additional hardship, they eventually made their way to Fort Hall in southeastern Idaho.

By 1870 the Blackfeet population had been decimated by European-introduced diseases, especially smallpox. Major epidemics occurred in

1781, 1837 and 1869–70. It is estimated that 6,000 Blackfeet, or two-thirds of the entire population, succumbed in the 1837 epidemic alone.[126] Osborne Russell's account of a meeting with a band of Blackfeet in 1838 serves as an example. In 1835 the trappers had been viciously attacked by the Blackfeet while on the Madison River just north of Henry's Lake and, upon discovering this encampment of about fifteen lodges, they decided to take revenge and

> smite it without leaving one to tell their fate. . . . but when within about 2 miles of the village we met six of them coming to us unarmed who invited us in the most humble and submissive manner to their village to smoke and trade. This proceeding conquered the bravest in our camp. For we were ashamed to think of fighting a few poor Indians nearly dwindled to skeletons by the small Pox and approaching us without arms.[127]

The Blackfeet were further demoralized in January 1870 by the Baker Massacre on the Marias River in which 173 Piegan Indians were killed and a large number captured. Lt. Gustavus C. Doane was " . . . the first and last man in [the] Piegan camp January 23, 1870 . . . [and called it the] . . . greatest slaughter of Indians ever made by U.S. troops." Prisoners included 140 women and children who, when it was suspected they were infected with smallpox, were released with no food, shelter, or other provisions to fend for themselves in January on the Montana plains.[128] This event marked the end of Blackfeet hostility.

Although down, the Blackfeet were not out. Since 1870 most Blackfeet have lived on their respective reservations in northern Montana and southern Alberta on the border of Glacier and Waterton National Parks. Following the designation of Glacier Park in 1910, the Blackfeet found themselves again in conflict with Anglos—this time over hunting and fishing rights and place names.[129] While battling over hunting rights in the newly formed park, the Blackfeet, with the encouragement of Louis Hill of the Great Northern Railroad, became a highly-publicized symbol of Glacier National Park.[130] They quickly learned that the growing tourist trade could be a source of income. For several decades up until the 1940s Blackfeet peddled curios and posed for photographs along the highways and around Park hotels. This pattern changed in the 1950s. The new generation of Blackfeet were more interested in real jobs. Some were employed as rangers, but more often they drove trucks and tended camps. Park Service–Blackfeet relations in the 1990s tended more toward tribal leaders presenting programs on Blackfeet culture.[131]

Crow

Crow Indians were recent arrivals in the territory along the Yellowstone River. They left the Hidatsa farming villages on the Missouri River in North Dakota about 1776 and arrived in southern Montana shortly thereafter. Horses were undoubtedly acquired before the move and by the time they settled in Montana, the Crow were well established in the Plains lifestyle.[132] The Crow, like the Hidatsa, spoke a Siouan[133] language and their name for themselves, *Ap sar roo kai*, actually refers to anything that flies.[134] The Crow were known for flamboyant horsemanship and their beautiful and distinctive styles of decorating clothing and accouterments with beads and porcupine quills.

Osborne Russell had numerous encounters with Crow Indians while trapping and traveling through the country east of Yellowstone. A number of those experiences were confrontational, as the Crow were known as skillful thieves. Nonetheless, he describes the Crow people at length in positive terms, characterizing them as "tall well proportioned and handsomely featured."[135]

The Crow occasionally traveled through the Park on hunting or raiding excursions. In 1870 the Langford-Washburn party, on their historic visit to Yellowstone, encountered a group of 100 Crow Indians near Bottler Ranch on the Yellowstone River in the northern portion of the Park. In 1877 Lt. Gustavus Doane lived with the Crow Indians on the Big Horn River in southern Montana and commanded a group of Crow scouts. These scouts are described as "athletic young men, tall . . . and brave," burnished by the sun.[136] Although hostilities occurred, these Indians were known generally for their friendship with white Americans and often served as scouts for the army. The Crow Indian reservation is on the Yellowstone River in southern Montana.

Shortly after Yellowstone became a national park, Philetus Norris was concerned that the Park infringed on the Crow Reservation. The Fort Laramie Treaty of 1868 designated Crow lands as extending south to the 45th parallel, which included the narrow strip of land north of the Montana-Wyoming border that corresponds to that parallel. In 1880 the land was transferred to the Park.[137]

Supt. Horace Albright's close relationship with the Crow during his stay in Yellowstone (1919–1929) is described in Chapter 9.

Shoshone-Bannock

The people who most often lived in and visited Yellowstone in recent times were the Shoshone of southern Idaho, western Wyoming, and northwestern Utah, and the Bannock, who lived among, and are closely related to, the Shoshone of southeastern Idaho.

Linguistic studies and, in some cases, archaeology, indicate that the Shoshone arrived in this region fairly recently, perhaps as late as 1300.[138] The Shoshone, Northern Paiute, Ute, and Southern Paiute are all Numic speakers. Linguistic and archaeological evidence suggests that within the last 1,000 years, these people gradually moved north and east from southern California into and across the Great Basin.[139] They spoke a similar language and, for the most part, were hunters and gatherers.

The principal Shoshone groups near Yellowstone were the Lemhi Shoshone,[140] who lived in central Idaho's Lemhi Valley and Salmon River Mountains north of the Snake River Plain, the Northern Shoshone of southern Idaho and northern Utah, and the Eastern Shoshone of western Wyoming. All the Shoshone in the region were called "Snakes" by whites and neighboring tribes alike. The term is of uncertain origin.[141] The arrival of the horse in the 1700s served to differentiate the groups. Those who had access to grasslands to support horse herds became equestrian hunters who regularly crossed the Rockies to hunt bison. Those who were not mounted were often referred to as Diggers, a term also applied to other Great Basin, Columbia Plateau, and California Indians. This term derives from the importance of root crops (which had to be dug) in the diet of these peoples.[142]

Great Basin Indians, including the Shoshone, followed a tradition of referring to certain groups after a particular food that was important to them and common in the area where they lived. For example, the Shoshone living on the plains where bison were abundant were called *Kutzundika* or "Buffalo Eaters," while those living along the salmon-rich Snake River drainage were referred to as *Agaidika*, "Salmon Eaters."[143] There were also Rabbit Eaters, Pine Nut Eaters, and Sheepeaters. Therefore, any of these Numic speakers who made mountain sheep an important part of their diet were likely to be called Sheepeaters.

Figure 18. Bannock family group. (William H. Jackson, photographer, YNP Photo Archives, Neg. No. YELL 10115.)

Ethnographer Catherine Fowler has argued that, among other things, the names were a signal to those living outside the region where certain eaters lived that those people had such resources to share.[144]

The Lemhi Shoshone blended with the Idaho Sheepeaters, who lived in the mountainous headwaters of the Salmon River. The arrival of the horse enticed some of these Shoshone to put their stock into bison hunting; others retained the more traditional Sheepeater lifestyle. By far the most famous of the Lemhi is Sacajewea, who served as a guide for Lewis and Clark. She was captured by the Blackfeet in 1800 at the Three Forks of the Missouri in Montana while hunting bison.[145]

The Bannock are a group of Northern Paiute who most likely migrated to southern Idaho in the 1600s or 1700s.[146] The Northern Paiute closest to the Bannock at the time of European contact were 200 miles west in Oregon. The reasons for the presence of a group of Northern Paiute among the Northern Shoshone are not known but may be a result of the Bannock moving east as the numbers of bison diminished in the northwestern Great Basin. Regardless, when the first explorers entered Idaho, the Bannock were in place, and they remain there today with the Northern Shoshone on the Fort Hall reservation.

The etymology of the name Bannock is, like Snake, difficult to trace. The term is most likely derived from the Bannocks' name for themselves, *Banakwut* or, as the Fort Hall Shoshone referred to them, *Ba naite*. The latter translates as "people from below."[147] Perhaps of most importance is that, despite the linguistic differences, the Bannock and the Northern Shoshone of southern Idaho got along well together. They intermarried, traveled together, and were usually bilingual, speaking both Shoshone (Central Numic) and Bannock (Western Numic). The Bannock language has slowly given way to Shoshone, primarily because there are more Shoshone.[148] In 1950 one person in ten on the Fort Hall Reservation claimed Bannock descent. Both had adopted the horse by the early 1700s and were committed to the Plains way of life. Bison, however, were never as plentiful west of the Rockies as they were on the vast prairies, and treks over the mountains were necessary after about 1840 when the herds in the Snake River Plains disappeared.[149] These trips often took them through Yellowstone.

Even after the adoption of the horse the Shoshone-Bannock continued to follow many old patterns. They spent winters along the Snake River near Fort Hall between present-day Pocatello and Blackfoot. In the spring and early summer they traveled west down the river to Shoshone Falls (the farthest point salmon could travel up the Snake River) and to Big Camas Prairie north of Twin Falls. They obtained salmon and camas on these trips, partially through trade with other Shoshone groups and partially by gathering the foods themselves (see Chapter 7 for more on Big Camas Prairie). In the later summer the treks to the bison country began. Routes taken include the Bannock Trail (described in Chapter 5) through Targhee Pass and Yellowstone Park, over Rea's Pass down the Madison River to the Three Forks of the Missouri in Montana, and south of the Yellowstone/Grand Teton region into southwestern Wyoming where they joined with the Wind River Shoshone. The Lemhi Shoshone usually traveled over the Lemhi Pass and past current Virginia City and Bozeman to get to the hunting grounds.

Many spent the winter in Montana, where the climate was sometimes milder than in the Snake River area and where they could hunt for a few weeks in the spring. Others returned to Idaho in the fall and lived on the meat obtained in Montana and other stores gathered during the year. This pattern of long-range movement practiced by the mounted Shoshone was quite different from that of the Sheepeaters of the Salmon River and Yellowstone country.

4

The Sheepeaters

The Sheepeaters made their homes in the high mountain plateaus and valleys of Yellowstone Park, the Wind River Mountains of Wyoming, and the Lemhi Fork of the Salmon River in central Idaho. Although these mountain dwellers were all called Sheepeaters, they were united only by a common language, their preference for their mountain homeland, and the primary big-game animal in those areas, the bighorn sheep. The following discussion draws on the Sheepeater literature for all these areas.

The Shoshone term for Sheepeaters was *Tukaduka* or *Tukarika,* meaning literally "sheep" (*tuka* or *tukku*) "eater" (*rika*).[150] The Sheepeaters of Yellowstone were also referred to as *Toyani* or "mountain dwellers" by other Shoshone groups.[151] Some scholars have suggested that *Toyani* refers to the groups that lived solely in the mountains, while *Tukarika* refers to more migratory groups. More colorful names include *Tonkey,* a term used by the Cook-Folsom party to refer to "friendly Sheepeaters" encountered near the northern boundary of the Park as they traveled up the Yellowstone River in 1869.[152]

Sheepeaters probably arrived in the Yellowstone Park area as late as 1800.[153] As discussed in Chapter 3, the Sheepeaters spoke Uto-Aztekan like other Shoshone of Idaho and, like them, were perhaps part of the northeastern movement of Uto-Aztekan (Numic) peoples across the Great Basin discussed in Chapter 3.

Early Impressions

The earliest reports of Sheepeaters come from the explorers and trappers who penetrated the Rocky Mountains in the early 1800s.[154] In 1811 the Hunt party bound for Astoria, Oregon, crossed the Rockies just south of the Grand Tetons and camped at Alexander Henry's abandoned

Figure 19. Family group of Shoshone Indians (perhaps Sheepeaters or Salmon-eaters) encamped near head of Medicine Lodge Creek, Idaho, 1871. [William H. Jackson, photographer, Bureau of American Ethnology, Smithsonian Institution, Neg. No. 1713.]

post near present-day St. Anthony, Idaho. A Shoshone Indian and his son visited the camp and are described in typical ethnocentric fashion:

> On the 14th day [of October], a poor, half-naked Snake Indian, one of that forlorn caste called the Shuckers, or Diggers, made his appearance at the camp. He came from some lurking-place among the rocks and cliffs, and presented a picture of that famishing wretchedness to which these lonely fugitives among the mountains are sometimes reduced.[155]

About 25 years later, in 1835, Capt. Benjamin Bonneville crossed the Wind River Mountains of Wyoming and encountered three Sheepeaters who were described in a similar tone:

> Captain Bonneville at once concluded that these belonged to a kind of hermit race, scanty in number, that inhabit the highest

and most inaccessible fastness. They speak the Shoshone language and probably are offsets from that tribe, though they have peculiarities of their own, which distinguish them from all other Indians. They are miserably poor, own no horses, and are destitute of every convenience to be derived from an intercourse with the whites. Their weapons are bows and stone pointed arrows, with which they hunt the deer, the elk and the mountain sheep. They are to be found scattered about the countries of the Shoshones, Flathead, Crow and Blackfeet tribes, but their residences are always in lonely places and the clefts of rocks.[156]

Bonneville's account is balanced by a more informative description in the journal of the literate and highly active trapper Osborne Russell. Russell encountered this group of Sheepeaters in the Lamar River Valley of the Park in 1835.

Here we found a few Snake Indians comprising six men, seven women and eight or ten children who were the only inhabitants of this lonely and secluded spot. They were all neatly clothed in dressed deer and sheepskins of the best quality and seemed to be perfectly happy. They were rather surprised at our approach and retreated to the heights where they might have a view of us without apprehending any danger, but having persuaded them of our pacific intentions we succeeded in getting them to encamp with us. Their personal property consisted of one old butcher knife, nearly worn to the back, two shattered fusees which had long since become useless for want of ammunition, a small stone pot and about 30 dogs on which they carried their skins, clothing, provisions, etc. on their hunting excursions. They were well armed with bows and arrows pointed with obsidian.[157]

Shortly after the establishment of Yellowstone as a national park, Supt. P. W. Norris described the natives of the region:

These sheepeaters were very poor, nearly destitute of horses and firearms, and, until recently, even of steel or iron hatchets, knives, or other weapons or implements. The stumps and the ends of the poles for lodges, wickeups [sic], and coverts for arrow-shooting, from having been cut by their rude obsidian or volcanic-glass axes, appear not unlike beaver-gnawings. . . . On account of this lack of tools they constructed no permanent habitations, but as evidenced by traces of smoke and fire-brands they dwelt in caves and nearly inaccessible niches in the cliffs, or in skin-covered lodges, or in circular upright brush-heaps called wickeups, decaying evidences of which are abundant near the Mammoth Hot springs, the various fire-hole basins, the shores of Yellowstone Lake, the newly explored Hoodoo region, and in nearly all of the sheltered glens and valleys of the Park.[158]

A half-century later Swedish anthropologist Ake Hultkrantz described the Sheepeaters of Yellowstone Park in one of his several papers on the Shoshone of Wyoming and Idaho:

These were mixed with Bannock, and were therefore called by the Shoshoni in other quarters *panaiti toyani* (Bannock mountain dwellers). Judging from the available evidence the *tukudika* have comprised partly an old layer of Shoshoni "walkers," who still retained the mode of life from the period before the introduction of the horse, and who established a culture specialized to suit mountain conditions, and partly impoverished Plains Shoshoni who had lost their horses or who had from fear of the powerful Algonkian and Siouan tribes been obliged to abandon the life on the plains.[159]

Still another account is offered by noted anthropologist Sven Liljeblad, whose description counters the notion that the people were impoverished. He states, "the mountaineers [Sheepeaters] were much better off than other Shoshoni, save the buffalo hunters." They were big-game hunters and "the most skilled hunters on foot of all Idaho Indians."[160] He further states that to describe the Sheepeaters as a people who either did not have access to horses or had lost them misrepresents the situation. Many Idaho Sheepeaters (and this logically would apply to those in the Yellowstone area also) chose not to be mounted simply because "horses would have been more trouble than gain."[161] Horses brought the danger of horse-stealing raids and the trouble of dealing with them in rough, heavily forested terrain.

Among these several descriptions is a common thread that describes the Sheepeater way of life during the period just before European contact. The following sections depict the Sheepeater culture by comparing these disparate sources.

Lifeway

During the century or so that they inhabited the Yellowstone region, the Sheepeaters lived in the traditional manner of their Great Basin ancestors. The year was divided into a time-proven pattern of movements designed to coincide with the availability of principal food items. This annual round was followed by small camp groups consisting of two to five families in proportions much like that described above by Osborne Russell.

The annual round in Yellowstone was related primarily to two seasons, summer and winter. Summer found the Shoshone high in the mountains pursuing mountain sheep. The meat was preferred by all Indians of this region, and the sheepskins provided raw materials for clothing and accessories. Rams' horns were used to make special tools. Summer was also a time for fishing and gathering various greens, roots, and berries as they ripened. Birds, such as mountain grouse and waterfowl, and many small mammals, including beaver, marmot, ground squirrel, and porcupine were available in considerable numbers in the summer. The pursuit of these foodstuffs would have occasionally carried the Sheepeaters out of the mountains into the lower river valleys along the Yellowstone, Madison, and Snake Rivers or into the Henry's Lake region, where they would have met the Bannock who often spent time there. Camps during the snow-free period were of short duration since the Indians moved on a tight schedule, following the pattern of food availability.

During the winter, camps were semi-permanent. The Sheepeaters settled in some sheltered creek or river bottom with convenient access to fuel, fresh water, and yarding elk, sheep, deer, and bison.

The research of archaeologist Gary Wright and his colleagues in the Jackson Hole region offers some additional perspectives on the Sheepeater yearly cycle. As noted in Chapter 2, they found evidence that argues strongly for the importance of plant foods in the lives of the people who occupied the region from about 6,000 years ago to just up to the Historic period.[162] In this ancient pattern, which Wright calls a high-country adaptation, people moved with the seasons from lower to higher elevations following the ripening root plants, especially blue camas, as they became available. Base camps were located in the meadows where these plants flourished. In large part, this scheduled upward

Figure 20. Shoshone encampment at Fort Washakie about 1890. The brush structures on the left resemble the wickiups traditionally made by Great Basin people and the Sheepeaters. (Photograph by Throsser (?), Neg. No. P80, Photo Archives, Brigham Young University, Provo, Utah.)

movement coincided with that of large game, especially sheep, and ended at base camps around 8,000 feet. As fall approached, gathering shifted to berries, and people moved down toward the wintering grounds of bighorn sheep and elk.[163] This model is based on extensive survey and archaeological excavations in the Jackson Hole region.

Interestingly, Wright describes this high-country pattern as disappearing about 150 years before the Sheepeaters arrived in the area. Like their Great Basin cousins, the Sheepeaters were more focused on arid lands and seed exploitation than on roots.[164] He also argues that the Sheepeaters were more intent on summertime sheep hunting, providing an additional contrast with the earlier pattern. Because there are no written records, it is difficult to know whether these strategy shifts were due to replacement of peoples, internal change, or some independent factor such as shifts in resource availability. Such fascinating questions about early history rely almost solely on the archaeological record.

Sheepeater groups traveling together were likely families related by blood or marriage. The Sheepeaters traveled on foot using dogs as pack animals or carried their belongings on their backs. Dog travois were commonly employed during their moves. The number of camp groups frequenting the Yellowstone Park area is not known, but estimates range from as low as six to as many as fifteen, and suggest that the total Yellowstone Sheepeater population was between 150 and 400. W. H. Jackson, the famous frontier photographer who visited the Park in 1871 with the Hayden expedition, states that there were 340 Sheepeaters "living a retired life in the Mountains dividing Idaho from Montana."[165] This figure would most likely have included Sheepeaters in Yellowstone and in the Lemhi River drainage of Idaho. The Indian agents at Lemhi reported 300 Sheepeaters in 1876 and 184 in 1878, an estimate that would not have included the Yellowstone population.[166]

Social, Political, Ceremonial Life

Understanding of the social and political organization of the Sheepeaters and mountain people is based on documented patterns among the Shoshone and Bannock of southern Idaho generally.[167] For the unmounted Sheepeaters, social and political structures were simple, and families were the most important social unit. Each group was led by a headman whose tenure lasted only as long as he could provide success in hunting and defending against enemies.[168] Special events such as an antelope and mountain sheep hunt, or hunting in general, occasionally called for a special chief who presided over that activity. These positions were temporary. Within age and sex groupings, individuals were essentially equal in status. Families joined together for group activities when and where food or other critical resources were abundant or during the cold months of the year where food was cached.[169] (See Chapter 6 on the Bannock War and Big Camas Prairie for more on this.)

Important life events paralleled aging. The social group marked birth, coming of age or puberty, marriage, child raising, and death to recognize change and new status, although celebrations of these events were weakly developed.[170] Birth customs revolved around maintaining the health and well-being of both mother and father, and certain behaviors and food items were taboo to both during pregnancy. The burial of the afterbirth, umbilical cord, and milk teeth insured the welfare of the child. A female relative assisted the mother in childbirth in a small house especially constructed for that purpose.

The occasion of a young woman reaching menarche resulted in her isolation in a house similar to the birthing hut. The girl would usually be accompanied by her mother or maternal grandmother, who provided instruction in good behavior. This would include being industrious, advice reinforced by running or other vigorous activities, and fetching water or wood. The importance of these activities varied from group to group. Little evidence exists of a boy's puberty rites.[171]

Marriage was an informal social and economic union that bound a man and woman together to insure survival. Preferred marriages were between a man and his pseudo cross-cousin (his maternal aunt's or uncle's stepdaughter) and marriage of brothers of one family to sisters of another. If a man's brother died, he married the widow, thereby insuring care for her and his nieces and nephews.[172] Wives were also obtained by abduction of an unmarried, or even a married, girl. Newlyweds among the Lemhi Shoshone usually lived with or near the husband's family,[173] a pattern logically related to the importance of hunting with the Lemhi and their mountain-dwelling Sheepeater neighbors.

A division of tasks by sex was common in most hunter-gatherer societies and appeared to apply to the Sheepeaters also. Men hunted, provided defense, did heavy chores, and cared for hunting-related tools. Women cared for the home, gathered plant foods, and prepared the meals. Relatives such as grandparents often lived with the family and assisted in rearing children and doing small chores.

Death rites were influenced by the general concerns about spirits and power that pervaded Numic cosmology. When an adult died, family members dressed the individual in best clothes before burying the corpse in the mountains. Preferred locations for burials were rocky slopes. Ideally, the house where the person lived and his/her belongings were burned. Relatives often retained more valuable possessions. The burning of the house and belongings allowed the spirit of the deceased to depart rather than linger nearby. The living feared the dead and believed the deceased would try to take them along to the Land of the Dead. Afterlife was thought to be happy and in a place filled with an abundance of a group's favorite food.[174]

Religious beliefs were not formal, yet they permeated the lives of the Shoshone, including the Sheepeaters.[175] Nature was central, and animals with human-like qualities such as speech populated sacred stories. Wolf, coyote, weasel, and bear possessed powers for luck and success in war; eagle and beaver were important for curing.[176] Power or *poha*, obtained through dreams while sleeping in sacred places (especially in the mountains), gave luck in hunting, gambling, and especially curing. Power could be obtained through appeal to the supernatural through the Sun Dance, sleeping in sacred places, or through prayers. Julian Steward's Fort Hall Shoshone informants reported that power could be obtained at Soda Springs in eastern Idaho.[177] Dinwoody Canyon on the Wind River Reservation was considered particularly sacred and powerful. Canyon rock art depicts important beings such as Water Ghost and Rock Ghost.[178] These beings were feared because they could cause sickness and even death. Other feared beings included water babies—often associated with springs—and the mountain dwarf.[179]

Great Basin shamans were *puhagunt*, religious healers who relied on an intimate knowledge of certain curative plants and an ability to remove foreign objects or restore souls through power obtained in dreams. Removal of objects required a sucking tube; soul restoration involved trances to allow the shaman's soul to search the lost soul of the sick individual.[180] Shamans also played critical roles in hunting antelope and perhaps mountain sheep. Both animals were obtained through communal drives. Western Shoshone shamans were responsible for "charming" the animals into drive lines and catch corrals.[181] Archaeologists studying the drive lines aimed to capture the bighorns in the mountainous regions east of Yellowstone have found evidence of shamanistic activity. They discovered small log structures integrated into the drive lines and concluded they most likely functioned as a place for a shaman to lure the animals into the trap.[182] All of the traps dated were used within the last several hundred years. Additional evidence of shamanism revolving around hunting mountain sheep are skulls of large rams placed in trees. Often the brain case was opened, an act considered further evidence of ritual behavior.[183] Although undated, the ram skulls, a number of which are documented in northwest Wyoming, are thought to be associated with native peoples living there in the recent past. These remains point to the importance of mountain sheep to early peoples and the integration of religion into hunting activities.

The most important ceremonies were dances. Circle dances were the most common among Great Basin peoples and the Father or Shuffling

Dance was considered a Sheepeater tradition.[184] This was a nocturnal affair held in the fall, winter, or spring, with men and women participating. Such events were eagerly anticipated as a time of socializing and communal bonding. They were also supplications to beings who could bring blessings to the participants.

Houses

Sheepeater shelters probably took several forms and followed the pattern of their unmounted Shoshone-speaking cousins in the Great Basin. Foremost of these was the domed willow or brush wickiup, constructed by placing a number of small, pliable poles in a circle 10 to 15 feet in diameter, bending them into the center, and tying the tops together to form a hogan or igloo shape. This superstructure was covered with slabs of bark, hides, or sheaves of grass that may have been secured with encircling withes of willow tied into place. A hole in the center of the roof let smoke escape, and a doorway was placed opposite the prevailing wind. Winter structures were more substantial, with walls reinforced with logs, stones, and earth piled around the perimeter for protection from the cold. Usually two families shared one wickiup.

Another important structure was a sort of windbreak made by planting a semicircle of poles in the ground and piling branches against them as protection from the strong winds that blow in the Rocky Mountains. This roofless shelter could be erected quickly by a small group of people and was ideal for use during summer, when camps were moved frequently. Variations on this windbreak and the domed wickiup were sometimes combined with the face of a cliff or rock overhang.

Several conical wickiups consisting of up to 100 poles placed in a tipi-like circle have been discovered in Yellowstone and attributed to the Sheepeaters. However, these structures were not in the Shoshone tradition; they more closely resemble war lodges erected by the Crows who occasionally traveled in Yellowstone Park.[185]

Clothing and Crafts

According to Osborne Russell, the clothing worn by the Sheepeaters consisted of beautifully tanned elk, deer, or sheep skins that were used for shirts and leggings. The beauty of these tanned skins was the

Figure 21. Park Ranger Wayne Replogle standing beside wickiup on Wickiup Creek in Yellowstone. (D. Condon, photographer, YNP Photo Archives, Neg. No. YELL 37836.)

result of using two brains per hide rather than one, which was the norm for most Indian tannings.[186] Women's dresses were made from two carefully tanned mountain-sheep hides. Tough badger and elk skins were made into hunters' moccasins, while soft deer skins were made into more comfortable footwear. Fox and coyote skin with the fur left on was used for hats and leggings, and tanned antelope skins were lined with rabbit fur to make warm blankets. The most highly prized blankets were of wolf skin, which symbolized the hunter's skill and the tanner's art and were highly sought after during trade events.[187] Russell "obtained a large number of elk, deer and sheep skins from them [Sheepeaters] of the finest quality and three neatly dressed panther skins in return for awls axes kettles tobacco ammunition etc."[188]

The Sheepeaters also excelled at making bows from the horns of various animals. According to Russell, "the bows were beautifully wrought from Sheep, Buffalo and Elk horns secured with Deer and Elk sinews and ornamented with porcupine quills and generally about 3 feet long." These powerful composite bows were made from the thick ridges on the upper side of the sheath of a ram's horn by heating it to make it pliable and then straightening it. Excess was trimmed off and the piece was heated and shaped until a tapered piece 18 to 24 inches long, an inch thick at the butt, and oval in cross-section remained. An identical piece was fashioned from the other horn. The two ends were then carefully beveled, fitted together, and joined by laying a short, separate piece of horn over the joint. The joint was then tightly wrapped with wet rawhide. The bow was further strengthened by gluing strips of animal sinew to the back.[189] Such a bow took two months to make and could send an arrow completely through a bison. Small wonder that they were highly prized by the Sheepeaters and other groups, who would give a horse and a gun for a good one.[190]

Other weapons and tools important to the Sheepeaters were arrows tipped with small, side-notched points, stone knives and scrapers for butchering game and processing hides, and stone pots for cooking. Arrows were sometimes tipped with a poison made from the roots of local plants to ensure hunter success.[191]

Although stone pots are rather heavy for nomadic people to carry from place to place and were undoubtedly often cached, we do know from Russell's first-hand description that some groups carried stone bowls with them. These stone pots may be like the steatite vessels pictured in Chapter 2, as the shape of these vessels is similar to those probably made by the Shoshone during the last 500 years. Heavily used steatite quarries, near which caches of vessel blanks have been found, are known within the traditional territory of the Sheepeaters—the Wind River, Teton, and Big Horn ranges of Wyoming.[192]

By the early 1800s the Sheepeaters had access to trade goods such as glass trade beads, buckets, guns, ammunition, and metal for knives,

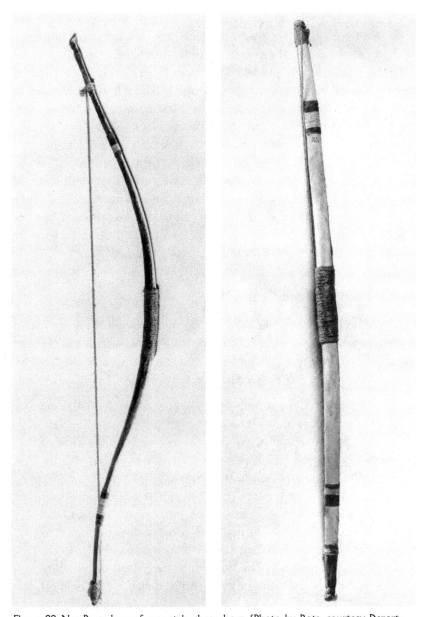

Figure 22. Nez Perce bow of mountain-sheep horn. (Photo by Rota, courtesy Department Library Services, Neg./Trans. No. 324352, American Museum of Natural History, Cat. No. 1/2707.)

axes, awls, and arrow and spear points. Russell's description makes it clear that these exotic items were available, but only in limited numbers, and probably did not affect their lifestyle. The Sheepeaters used stone grinding implements to process plant foods. Seeds and nuts were placed on flat, smoothed stones and ground into a coarse flour to be used in mushes, using bun-shaped hand stones. Berries, roots, and meat were pounded in a stone bowl (mortar) with an elongate stone (pestle). Like the steatite pots, these heavy tools were often left at camps to be used during subsequent stops. Digging sticks were used to unearth roots. These were carefully made from strong elastic woods such as mountain mahogany or serviceberry and were sharpened and fire-hardened. They were sometimes padded on the upper end with a crosspiece of bone or elk antler affixed to provide a handle. Well-made digging sticks were prized by women, who did most of the root gathering.[193]

Food and Food Getting

Sheepeater hunting practices did not rely solely on the use of the bow and arrow. In their pursuits of large game, such as the bighorn sheep, they constructed elaborate timber traps to capture several animals at once. P. W. Norris describes the traps:

> Other traces of this tribe are found in the rude, decaying, and often extensive pole and brush fences for drive-ways of the deer, bison, and other animals, to the narrow-coverts, in the canyons or in the narrow passes between them, for slaughter with the rude lances and obsidian-headed arrows.
> For want of proper tools, but little timber was cut, and these drive-ways were mainly constructed of the ever-abundant dead and fallen saplings, with the roots attached, which, from their pitchy properties, long outlast the trunks and branches, thus enabling an experienced mountaineer to trace these drive-ways a long distance, even in groves of thrifty timber. . . . Countless drive-ways and coverts in every state of decay are still found in favorable localities throughout the Park, and are often crossed unobserved by ordinary tourists.[194]

Similar game traps outside the Park in the Wind River, Absaroka, and other mountain ranges east of Yellowstone have been archaeologically

Figure 23. Remains of a mountain sheep trap in the Wind River Mountains. (George C. Frison, *Prehistoric Hunters of the High Plains*, Academic Press.)

investigated and show mountain-sheep bones in the catch pen, leaving little doubt as to the intended quarry.[195] Fences more than 10 feet high were constructed with an inward lean to prevent sheep from jumping or clambering over the top.

Hunters also ambushed their prey at known haunts, such as salt or mineral licks, or narrow saddles through which game trails passed. Dogs were sometimes used to assist in hunting large game. Snowshoes were worn in the winter so the hunter could run quickly over the snow while hoofed animals such as sheep and elk would bog down. Elk were occasionally shot at night when the animals visited mineral deposits to "lick the clay."[196]

Fish, especially trout and whitefish, were abundant in certain areas of Yellowstone and were caught and eaten by the Sheepeaters. Fishing was done mostly with spears and snares, especially during the spawning runs in late spring and early summer. Nets and wires apparently were not used.[197] Along the edge of Yellowstone Lake, however, there are alignments of stone that may have functioned as part of a fish trapping system constructed by peoples who lived in Yellowstone before the Sheepeaters.

Vegetable foods played a major role in the Sheepeaters' diet. Ripening roots, seeds, nuts, and berries probably played a more important role in determining when the Sheepeaters moved to their next camping area than the availability of game did. The harvest season was short, and careful attention had to be paid to the plants' stages of development, or the seed would ripen and drop, or the berries would be quickly eaten by birds, bears, or other fruit-lovers. Game was less predictable and the timing of hunts less critical. Berries, such as huckleberries, raspberries, chokecherries, serviceberries, and various greens, bulbs, and roots were picked in season. Roots were an especially important food to the prehistoric peoples of the Great Basin, Idaho, Oregon, and Washington. Yamp, bitterroot, tobacco root, and camas were gathered and eaten in the spring when the roots were new and succulent, or later in the fall when they were bigger. Camas grew in abundance in regions like Big Camas Prairie in southern Idaho and in other meadowlands such as Henry's Lake flats just west of the Park, Jackson Lake south of Yellowstone, and in certain locales in Yellowstone.[198] These roots were dug with sharpened sticks, cleaned, then baked in earth ovens for several days. They were then eaten or pounded, cooked more, dried, and stored for consumption during the cold and often lean winter months. Berries were likewise ground and dried in small cakes and stored. They provided a popular seasoning ingredient for otherwise bland mushes made from the ground seeds or nuts. Ants and grubs were also on the Sheepeater menu and were generally roasted before eating.

Like the piñon pine, which produces nuts in abundance for the Great Basin Indians, limber pine (*Pinus flexilis*) produced nuts in quantity.[199] These nuts were collected, then hulled and ground into a flour, which then was mixed with water to make mush.

Historic Period

Although the precontact history of the Sheepeaters is not well known, it is certain their way of life changed dramatically following the arrival of Europeans. Isolated, the Sheepeaters resisted change for some time. However, incursions of Plains groups into Yellowstone during the nineteenth century caused Sheepeaters to ally more closely with Washakie's band of Wind River Shoshone. This contact resulted in the acquisition of some horses and the amalgamation into fewer and larger bands. Some political unity was achieved during this time under head chief Toyaewowici.

After Yellowstone became a national park in 1872, the presence of Sheepeaters and other Native Americans was perceived as a potential deterrent to tourist traffic by Supt. P. W. Norris, especially after the Nez Perce campaign of 1877. To insure that Indians stayed out of Yellowstone, Norris worked hard to obtain an agreement with the Crow, Bannock, and Shoshone (including the Sheepeaters) that they would stay of of the Park.[200] In his 1881 Annual Report he alludes to this earlier effort and states his purpose:

> To prevent these forays [a reference to raids into the Park], in council at their agency on Ross Fork of Snake River, in Idaho, and in Ruby Valley, Montana, early in 1880, I obtained a solemn pledge from them to not thereafter go east of Henry's Lake, in Montana, or north of Hart Lake in Wyoming, to which . . . they faithfully adhered.[201]

This pledge was revisited in 1881 and further promises were obtained from agents to keep their wards out of the Park.

Despite Norris's efforts, the Sheepeaters continued to visit the area, but in a different capacity. Because of their detailed knowledge of the Park, the Sheepeaters were often employed as guides for government trips. For example, in August 1873 Capt. William A. Jones of the Corps of Engineers employed about fifteen Shoshones as part of his expedition to explore the potential for wagon routes from the Union Pacific Railroad to Yellowstone.[202] The most famous of these guides was Sheepeater Chief Togwatee, to whom Jones entrusted the route of his return trip. Togwatee took the party up the headwaters of the Yellowstone River, over Two Ocean Pass, and eventually through a small pass between the headwaters of the Wind and Snake Rivers. Jones named the pass "Togwatee" as a tribute to his guide. Togwatee's reputation was secure, and in 1882 he and several other Sheepeaters guided Gen. Philip Sheridan's exploration of parts of Wyoming, Idaho, and Montana.[203] In the late summer of 1883, Togwatee guided the grand entourage of President Chester A. Arthur. Togwatee and other Sheepeaters led the group over Indian trails as they traveled from Washakie Springs, up the Wind River and over the pass that now bears Togwatee's name, into Jackson Hole and then north into the Park. Chief Togwatee eventually became an important leader among the Wind River Shoshone and was also known for his skills as a shaman.[204]

Sheepeater War, 1879

A significant event in the history of the Sheepeaters on the Lemhi Reservation was the so-called Sheepeater War of 1879. Although the war occurred in central Idaho, it certainly affected the Yellowstone group. The war is typically described as beginning with the killing of five Chinese and two Anglos near Challis, Idaho, in February 1879. Some, however, have attributed the war in part to a change in attitude in the usually quiet Sheepeaters, as a consequence of Bannock War refugees joining with the Lemhi area Sheepeaters.[205] A series of minor raids on livestock occurred in the Indian Valley region and in the Weiser National Forest during the late summer and might have included Sheepeater participants. Much more serious was the death the previous summer of three men in Indian Valley when they pursued horse thieves. This action could also be attributed to repercussions from the Bannock War.

In April 1879, two white men were killed by Indians near Warren, Idaho. In May, Gen. O. O. Howard sent two detachments of soldiers to the Middle Fork of the Salmon, where they campaigned for four months. Neither detachment had much initial success in locating the "hostiles." Instead, the soldiers fought deep snow and treacherous, rough terrain for much of June and into July as they pursued the Shoshone over ground familiar to the Indians but not to the militia. Finally, on July 28, Lt. Henry Catley found the Sheepeaters—or they found him. Presumably, his Umatilla scouts informed him that they had spotted Indians, a report Catley ignored. Suddenly, on a cliff above the troops an Indian yelled and disappeared. Shots followed and two soldiers fell seriously wounded.[206] Catley wisely retreated and camped for the night. As the soldiers retreated the next day, they were attacked again and pinned down until nightfall. They fled after dark but lost twenty-three pack animals and all their supplies to the Sheepeaters.[207]

In August, presumably encouraged by Catley's defeat, the Indians attacked three men who were haying on their farm on the Middle Fork of the Snake. Ranch owner James Rains was killed and one of his friends seriously wounded.[208] General Howard urged that the efforts be stepped up, and Lt. Edward Farrow, another young officer, pressed the Indians, who abandoned some of their equipment. A skirmish resulted in the death of one soldier, causing the troops to stop their effort to rest men and horses. Farrow, second in command to Howard, sent the general a dispatch describing the soldiers' condition:

> The country is so rough that animals cannot be got through it at all. All our stock except a few of Captain Forse's horses and the animals captured by Farrow are exhausted. Most of our horses and mules have given out and have been shot.[209]

Finally, in September, Farrow encountered several Sheepeater women and children from whom he obtained information about the location of the Indian camp. But Indians eluded them once again. Shortly thereafter one of the Sheepeater chiefs approached the soldiers and surrendered, stating that he was tired of fighting. Farrow captured about sixty Sheepeaters, including fifteen "warriors."[210] According to Sven Liljeblad, the "armament of this formidable foe, pursued for three months by the United States Cavalry, mounted infantry, and enlisted Umatilla Scouts, totaled four carbines, one breech-loading and two muzzle-loading rifles, and one double-barreled shotgun."[211]

Conclusion

As a consequence of the Sheepeater War and Norris's earlier lobbying, most of the Sheepeaters of Yellowstone moved either to the Wind River Shoshone Reservation in Wyoming or the Fort Hall Shoshone-Bannock Reservation near Blackfoot, Idaho. Some probably also went to the Lemhi Reservation on the headwaters of the Salmon River. A number of the conservative Sheepeaters clung to the old ways, resisting the reservation until the turn of the last century.[212]

With the banning of all Indians from the Park, the region soon looked deserted. When General Sherman inspected the area in 1877, just before the Nez Perce War, he wrote, "We saw no signs of Indians." But as we shall see, the Park soon provided the setting for a portion of one of the most celebrated conflicts between the Indians and the U.S. Army—the Nez Perce War.

5

The Nez Perce War

In the spring and early summer of 1877 in the Wallowa Valley of eastern Oregon, a combination of events revolving around the attempts of the United States government to place the Nez Perce on a reservation culminated in an outbreak of hostilities between the Indians, the local settlers, and the military. After a series of small victories fought against U.S. troops, five of the Nez Perce bands, more or less united under the leadership of a chief named Looking Glass, decided their best chance for freedom lay in a retreat into Montana, where they could either find refuge with the Crows or flee into Canada. This Indian war had a lasting impact on the newly formed Yellowstone, the world's first national park.[213]

Battle of the Big Hole

About 200 men, 550 women and children, and more than 2,000 horses fled through the rugged Bitterroot Mountains and crossed over Lolo Pass southwest of Fort Missoula, Montana. After a brief skirmish with troops at "Fort Fizzle"[214] near Missoula, and perhaps feeling assured of their safety because of the friendly attitude of local whites, the Nez Perce slowed their retreat. The route they took, at the insistence of Looking Glass,[215] was southerly, much to the consternation of many of the warriors who wanted to turn north and escape into Canada.

Meanwhile, Gen. O. O. Howard, who was in charge of the pursuit of these "renegades," wired Fort Shaw, Montana, for troops to cut off the Nez Perce retreat while he followed their route over the Lolo Trail. Fort Shaw troops, led by Col. John Gibbon, moved quickly to overtake the Indians. Their numbers swelled to more than 250 when they were joined by the very settlers who had recently befriended the Nez Perce.

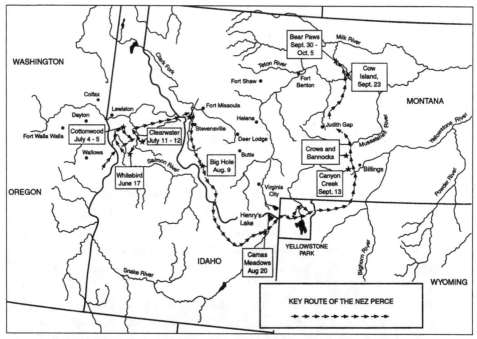

Figure 24. Route of Nez Perce flight during the 1877 war. (After Josephy 1965, 550–51.)

On the morning of August 9, 1877, the troops and settlers attacked the sleeping village of Nez Perce camped on the Big Hole River near Wisdom, Montana. The battle lasted throughout the hot summer day and by afternoon, Gibbon, who initially thought he would be an easy victor, found himself pinned down. He was eventually rescued by General Howard, but not before 29 of his soldiers were dead and 40 were wounded. Between 60 and 90 Nez Perce, mostly women and children, died at the Battle of the Big Hole. Twelve of their best warriors were killed, including the leaders Rainbow and Five Wounds.

Smarting from this loss, the Nez Perce bands fled south along the east slope of the divide under new leadership. Looking Glass, whose attitude had lulled them into a false sense of security, was out of favor. The new leader, Poker Joe, was half-French, half–Nez Perce and knew the Montana trails well. The angry Nez Perce crossed the divide into Idaho at Bannock Pass, raiding as they went, and met with Tendoy, chief of the Lemhi Shoshone, at the Lemhi Reservation near Junction, Idaho. The

Figure 25. A late-nineteenth-century photograph of Gen. Oliver Otis Howard. (Photograph from James A. Taylor's scrapbook, Bureau of American Ethnology, Smithsonian Institution, Neg. No. 77-13334.)

Shoshone wanted nothing to do with the Nez Perce. In fact, the Shoshone and Bannock at Fort Hall were anxious to do battle against them. General Howard had employed a contingent of Bannock scouts and allowed them to scalp the mutilated Nez Perce corpses at Big Hole. Eventually, the Nez Perce discovered that even their former confederates, the Crow and Cheyenne, had also become their enemies, so fickle were the alliances of Plains warrior groups.

The Flight East

Meanwhile, Howard joined Gibbon to head off the fleeing Indians by staying on the east side of the divide until he reached Monida Pass. Fearing the Indians would cross the Rockies and escape onto the Plains via the northern Yellowstone route, Howard sent forty troops on a shortcut through Centennial Valley to cut off the Nez Perce at Targhee Pass, just a few miles west of present-day West Yellowstone. Howard and the main body of soldiers, which had now been reinforced by fifty cavalry troops from Fort Ellis near Bozeman, camped at Camas Meadows in Idaho only a day behind the Indians. Here the Nez Perce took the offensive by doubling back and stealing 200 head of mules and generally harassing the army. Meanwhile, the troops at Targhee Pass, who had been unable to locate the Indians, became anxious and, thinking the Nez Perce had gone south through the Tetons, decided to rejoin Howard. Incredibly, these troops not only managed to miss seeing the Indians and their large horse herd but also managed to miss Howard, who arrived at Henry's Lake and Targhee Pass to find his troops gone and to discover the trail of the Nez Perce heading over the pass into Yellowstone.

By this time, the Nez Perce War had become a major news item on the East Coast. Indians were cast in the role of underdogs, and Howard was perceived as a pontifical, bungling general, who was continuously outwitted by the brilliant Nez Perce leader, Chief Joseph. Joseph was one of several chiefs and was not a war leader, but because of an initial misunderstanding by Howard at the outset of the war, Joseph had been described as the leader of the hostilities from the beginning. Gen. W. T. Sherman pressured Howard either to pursue the matter with vigor or give his command to a younger man. Stung by these remarks, Howard assured Sherman that he intended to persevere until the campaign concluded with the defeat of the Nez Perce.

Refreshed after three days' rest and inspired by his exchange with Sherman, Howard again took up the trail. Afraid that the arrival of the group of warlike Nez Perce on the Plains might stir up trouble among the recently subdued Sioux and other Plains groups, the army sent help. Two companies of Custer's old Seventh Cavalry led by Col. Samuel D. Sturgis were dispatched by Col. Nelson Miles to assist Howard in trapping the Nez Perce in Yellowstone. Lt. Gustavus C. Doane ascended the Yellowstone River from the north, while Sturgis skirted the Park and set

Figure 26. Thunder Coming From the Water Up Over the Land, Chief Joseph of the Nez Perce. (Charles M. Bell, photographer, Bureau of American Ethnology, Smithsonian Institution, Neg. No. 2906.)

up a blockade on the Clarks Fork River, where it was expected the Indians would appear. General Sherman had a change of heart and decided to transfer Howard's command to Lt. Col. C. C. Gilbert, then stationed at Fort Ellis. Ironically, Gilbert, bearing his letter of authorization, searched in vain through the Park for General Howard and, failing to find him, went home.

The Nez Perce War in Yellowstone

The Indian bands, under the direction of Poker Joe and unaware of all the hoopla, wisely decided against traveling the better-known and longer Bannock Trail (see Chapter 7). They chose instead a more direct route across the Park that took them up the Madison and Firehole Rivers. They eventually camped at the junction of the Firehole and Nez Perce Creek. Yellowstone had been a national park since 1872 and, incongruous as it may seem, there were tourists and other travelers there.

The Indians first encountered an old prospector named John Shively camped alone on the Firehole River a mile or so above Nez Perce Creek. As he ate supper, Shively was surrounded and captured by the Indians who, according to his later account, forced him into service as a guide.[216] Believing it unwise to refuse and knowing something of the country, he helped lead the Nez Perce through the Park for the next thirteen days before he escaped. According to Shively, the Indians were having a difficult time finding their way because they were south of the Bannock Trail.

Shively later told the tale of his adventure with the Nez Perce to James H. Mills, who recounted,

> There are from 600 to 800 Nez Perces in the band. Of these 250 are warriors but all will fight that can carry a gun. They have almost 2000 head of good average horses. Every lodge drives its own horses in front of it when traveling, each lodge keeping its band separate. The line is thus strung out so that they are three hours getting into camp. They are nearly all armed with repeating rifles, only half a dozen or so having muzzle loaders. They say they have more ammunition than they want. About one-sixth of the horses are disabled, lame or sore-backed, but they

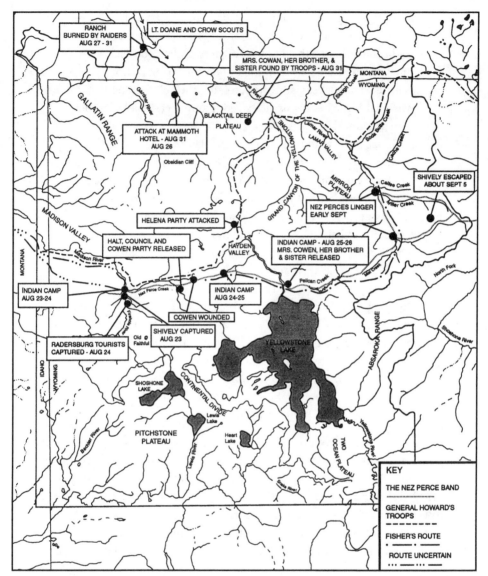

Figure 27. Nez Perce travels in Yellowstone during the war. (After M. Brown 1966 and Lang 1990.)

keep changing and hold all good horses in reserve. The horses are all in fair condition. They seemed at first anxious about the soldiers overtaking them but soon got over that, and had not intimation any troops were trying to intercept them in front. They kept up scouts ahead and after crossing the Yellowstone had no rear guard, only a few parties striking out occasionally on their own account.

So far as he could notice no particular chief seemed to be in command. All matters were decided in a council of several chiefs. White Bird was not known to him at all, as such, but thinks he was present in the councils in about a dozen of which Shively participated. Joseph is about thirty-five years of age, six feet high, and always in a pleasant mood, greeting him each time with a nod and smile. Looking Glass is 50 or 60 years old. He wears a white feather, and Joe Hale (Poker Joe) two, putting a new feather in his cap after Mr. Shivley [sic] joined them. They say they have lost 43 warriors altogether, of these 6 or 7 were killed in Norwood's fight near Camas Meadows, the remainder at Big Hole, where they lost many women and children. Joe Hale says he killed two soldiers there. They had but 10 or 12 wounded with them and one was dying when Shively escaped. They said they would fight soldiers but did not want to fight citizens—but Mr. S. (Shivley [sic]) says they will kill anybody.[217]

Later that same evening Nez Perce scouts discovered the campfire of nine tourists from Radersburg, Montana. The Indians captured the party the following morning to keep them from informing the army and dragged the entire group with them as they traversed the Central Plateau toward Hayden Valley. The Radersburg tourists, or Cowan party as it came to be known included Mr. and Mrs. George Cowan, Mrs. Cowan's brother and sister, Frank and Ida Carpenter, J. Albert Oldham, William Dingee, Charles Mann, A. J. Arnold, and D. L. Meyers. The tourists were treated relatively well at first, but as the day progressed, the younger warriors grew increasingly insolent and began exchanging their worn equipment for the tourists' newer and better saddles, guns, and horses.[218] Poker Joe was afraid trouble might break out and warned the members of the group that they should try to escape at the first opportunity. Two points seem clear from this action: first, the chiefs did not wish to harm the tourists; and second, the Indian leaders had little control over individual members of their following.

Shortly after Poker Joe gave his advice, two of the tourists, Dingee and Arnold, escaped. As a result some of the younger warriors lost their tempers and shot George Cowan first in the leg and then in the forehead, apparently killing him. Three other members of the party also escaped at this time. Cowan was left where he lay. His wife fainted. She and her hysterical sister, their brother, Shively, and a discharged soldier named James C. Irwin were dragged on to the Yellowstone River. The Indians later released everyone but Shively.[219] Mrs. Cowan published the story of the ordeal in several periodicals and described the moment when her husband was shot:

> Suddenly, without warning, shots rang out. Two Indians came dashing down the trail in front of us. My husband was getting off his horse. I wondered for what reason. I soon knew, for he fell as soon as he reached the ground—fell headlong down the hill. Shots followed and Indian yells, and all was confusion. In less time that it takes me to tell it, I was off my horse and by my husband's side, where he lay against a fallen pine tree. I heard my sister's screams and called to her. She came and crouched by me, as I knelt by his side. I saw he was wounded in the leg above the knee, and by the way the blood spurted out I feared an artery had been severed. He asked for water, I dared not leave him to get it, even had I been near. I think we both glanced up the hill at the same moment, for he said, "Keep quiet. It won't last long." That thought had flashed through my mind also. Every gun of the whole party of Indians was leveled on us three. I shall never forget the picture, which left an impress that years cannot efface. The holes in those guns barrels looked as big as saucers.
>
> I gave it only a glance, for my attention was drawn to something near at hand. A pressure on my shoulder was drawing me away from my husband. Looking back and up over my shoulder, I saw an Indian with an immense navy pistol trying to get a shot at my husband's head. Wrenching my arm from his grasp, I leaned over my husband, only to be roughly drawn aside. Another Indian stepped up, a pistol shot rang out, my husband's head fell back, and a red stream trickled down his face from

beneath his hat. The warm sunshine, the smell of blood, the horror of it all, a faint remembrance of seeing rocks thrown at his head, my sister's screams, a sick faint feeling, and all was blank.[220]

Cowan, apparently only stunned by the head wound, regained consciousness and began hobbling back toward their original camp. He was discovered by another Indian driving a small horse herd and shot again, this time in the hip. He was finally rescued by troops and treated by army physicians who, according to Cowan, were more interested in seeing the geysers than caring for his wounds. At the time of his rescue Cowan still had the bullet that had knocked him senseless sticking out of his forehead, just above his nose. He probably owed his life to wet powder or an improperly measured charge. Cowan was eventually reunited with his wife.

The only other member of the Radersburg party who was harmed was Oldham, who was shot through the cheek while escaping. He also survived, although he lost two teeth.

The route taken by the main body of Nez Perce has been a matter of some debate.[221] Accounts suggest they crossed the Yellowstone and headed up Pelican Creek, leaving three small groups of warriors behind to cover their flank and to slow the army. The party spread out as they passed through the grassy Pelican Valley, most likely to facilitate keeping track of the horse herd. They traveled northeast ascending the Pelican drainage and eventually descended to the headwaters of the Lamar River. Here they split into two groups, one group under Joseph heading down Mist Creek, and the other led by Looking Glass and Lean Elk making a short foray southeast and then down Cold Creek. Joseph's group traveled down to where Calfee Creek joins with the Lamar, while the larger group camped just below the Mist Creek–Lamar River juncture.[222] The Nez Perce were attracted by the grass-rich meadows along the upper Lamar River, reminiscent of their home country in Idaho and Oregon, and perhaps stayed there for several days. It is possible the decision to linger where grass and game were plentiful may have contributed to their eventual capture.[223]

In the Park near Hayden Valley were two other groups of tourists: the Earl of Dunraven, his friend Dr. George Kingsly, a guide named Texas Jack, and a wrangler; and the Helena or Weikert party, consisting of ten persons. Texas Jack discovered the Indians and escorted his party safely back to Mammoth Hot Springs but did not warn the other party about the Indians. The Helena party eventually discovered the Indians but, thinking they were out of harm's way, stayed in the Park. They camped that night on Otter Creek about three miles above the Upper Falls of the Yellowstone, still believing that there was no great danger and that they were hidden well enough. The next day, they were attacked by one of the scouting and raiding parties sent out to monitor military movements and determine the safest route out of the mountains.[224] One of their party, Charles Kenck, was killed on the spot and another, John Stewart, was wounded. The rest escaped unharmed, but they were split up. Several eventually gathered at the crude hotel at Mammoth Hot Springs. Two of the group, Joseph Roberts and seventeen-year-old August Foller, headed west and, after 30 or 40 miles of grueling travel, hit the Madison Valley and some of General Howard's supply wagons. After being fed by the soldiers, they headed down the river to Virginia City. At Mammoth, the hotel operator and some of the people headed for Bozeman. Five of the Helena party stayed behind to search for their missing companions.

Meanwhile, the Nez Perce scouting groups continued to harass civilians and military personnel in the Park, and roamed widely after attacking the Helena party. One warrior group traveled down the Yellowstone River valley to test it as a possible escape route. While there, they looted and burned the Henderson ranch a mile or so north of present-day Gardiner, Montana. At about this time troops under Lt. Gustavus Doane dispatched from Fort Ellis were moving up the Yellowstone Valley and, along with a contingent of Crow scouts, effectively cut off the Nez Perce route to the north. The Indians came by the Mammoth Hotel and discovered three of the remaining members of the Helena party. They killed Richard Dietrich, who had stayed behind to search for Foller, one of those who had fled to Virginia City. The warriors finally rejoined their families as the Indians prepared to descend onto the Plains.

Escape routes for the Indians were dwindling. As noted, Lieutenant Doane shut off the route down the Yellowstone, and General Howard continued to pursue from the rear. Howard's scouts, a group of forty or so Bannock under S. G. Fisher, were close on the Nez Perce heels, in some cases arriving at Indian camps shortly after the Indians left.[225] Unknown to the Indians, Col. S. D. Sturgis and more than 350 troops of the Seventh Cavalry waited on the Clarks Fork, a logical route to the

Montana Plains and, ultimately, Canada. The Shoshone River Valley, which lay more directly east, was unguarded but was a less direct route to freedom.

Despite their reticence to leave the lush Lamar Valley, the Indians eventually renewed their dramatic journey. After the raiding parties rejoined the Nez Perce bands, Joseph and his group followed one of the Bannock Trail routes up Miller Creek, while the larger group headed up the Lamar River. The two met near Hoodoo Basin.

General Howard was now confident of success. The Nez Perce would be cut off by Sturgis's command and be captured at last. There seemed to be no way out for the plucky group of Nez Perce, now surrounded in the mountains by the best of the Indian-fighting army. After Howard hacked a trail for his lumbering wagons and infantry through the central portion of the Park, he was north of the Indians. He traveled up the Lamar River to Soda Butte Creek, over to the headwaters of the Clarks Fork, and followed the highly visible Indian trail down the river toward the waiting Sturgis.

Nez Perce scouts apparently detected Sturgis lying in wait along the lower Clarks Fork. The Indian leaders, still headed by Poker Joe, decided upon a simple and perfectly conceived plan. Sturgis did not know where the Indians were and was worried that they might go south to the Shoshone River rather than down the nearly impassable Clarks Fork Canyon. The Nez Perce, in a well-executed move, made a highly visible start toward the Shoshone but then doubled back to the Clarks Fork. Sturgis and his troops moved south to the Shoshone River to block Indians who never arrived. By the time Sturgis discovered his mistake and found the Nez Perce trail leading back to the Clarks Fork, Howard was already ahead of him and the Nez Perce were 50 miles ahead of Howard.

The End of the Most Wonderful of Indian Wars

Heading down Clarks Fork, the Nez Perce turned toward the river's juncture with the Yellowstone. The flight now was north to Canada, freedom, and perhaps an alliance with Sitting Bull's Sioux. Shortly after crossing the Yellowstone west of present-day Billings, they fought a skirmish with Sturgis's troops and escaped. Harassed by Crow and Bannock scouts riding in advance of the military, the beleaguered

Nez Perce fled toward the Musselshell River, and crossed the Missouri at Cow Island. They raided a steamboat freight depot for food and fought off soldiers stationed there. Although Canada was now close, Looking Glass, who believed that the soldiers' pursuit was over, urged the bands to slow their pace to allow the families to rest. His advice was fatal.[226]

Col. Nelson Miles crossed the Missouri at the mouth of the Musselshell on a forced march from Fort Keogh and learned of the Nez Perce route. He caught the Indians camped at Snake Creek on the northern slopes of the Bear Paw Mountains 40 miles south of the Canadian border. The battle was intense and bloody and dragged on for six days. The Indians suffered terribly in the cold and from lack of food. Many of their chiefs, including Poker Joe and Looking Glass, were dead, and Howard and Sturgis had arrived with reinforcements. Ironically, Looking Glass was the last Indian killed in battle. Shortly after the council in which the Indians decided to abandon the fight, Looking Glass stood up to look at an approaching figure hoping it was a messenger from Sitting Bull, was hit in the forehead by a bullet, and died on the spot.[227] Shortly thereafter Joseph rode to meet with Howard and Miles.

> Tell General Howard I know his heart. What he told me before, I have in my heart. I am tired of fighting. Our chiefs are killed. Looking Glass is dead. Toohoolhoolzote is dead. The old men are all dead. It is the young men who say yes and no. He who led on the young men is dead. It is cold and we have no blankets. The little children are freezing to death. My people, some of them, have run away to the hills and have no blankets, no food; no one knows where they are—perhaps freezing to death. I want to have time to look for my children and see how many I can find. Maybe I shall find them among the dead. Hear me my chiefs. I am tired; my heart is sick and sad. From where the sun now stands I will fight no more forever.[228]

The "wonderful," senseless war was over. Chief Joseph and 431 of the Nez Perce surrendered. About 330 escaped into Canada. Colonel Miles demonstrated his respect for the Nez Perce in a letter to his wife by stating, "The fight was the most fierce of any Indian engagement I have ever been in. . . . The whole Nez Perce movement is unequaled in the history of Indian warfare."[229]

The Fate of the Nez Perce

Following the war, the fate of the Nez Perce paralleled that of other defeated Indians. It was a time of suffering and despair. Miles and Howard had promised the Nez Perce at the Bear Paw that they would return to their homes in Idaho and Oregon. Instead they were shipped to Fort Leavenworth, Kansas, where they stayed until the summer of 1878 when they were moved to the Quapaw Indian Reserve in Kansas. In June 1879 they were again relocated, this time to Tonkawa, Oklahoma, where they stayed until 1885 when they were finally allowed to return to the Northwest.[230]

It was during this postwar period that Joseph's reputation as a powerful spokesman and humanitarian rose to even greater heights. He tirelessly pursued the promises made by Miles to be allowed to return home. In January 1879 he visited Washington, D.C., spoke to a gathering of members of Congress and the Cabinet, and also met with the President of the United States. These efforts, coupled with the earlier media coverage of the war, elevated Joseph to a position of national prominence. Joseph's attempts to return his people to their homeland were complemented by those of his one-time enemy, Nelson Miles, who personally appealed to President Hayes on behalf of the Nez Perce. These combined efforts popularized the issue, and the appeal was supported by a number of eastern advocacy groups.

Finally, in 1885, Congress approved the return of the Nez Perce; however, the Commissioner of Indian Affairs argued convincingly that the settlers of the Wallowa Valley did not want Joseph's band to return because of several murders that occurred at the beginning of the war. As a result Joseph and his followers were sent to the Colville Reservation on Nespelem Creek in northeastern Washington, while the remainder of the Nez Perce went home to Lapwai. Until his death, Joseph appealed repeatedly to be allowed to return to his beloved Wallowa. All requests were denied. He died in 1904 in Nespelem while sitting in front of his tipi fire. The cause of death, according to the agency physician, was a broken heart.[231]

6

The Bannock War

Big Camas Prairie lies just north of the Snake River about 75 miles east of Boise, Idaho. It is a long, grassy valley blessed with flowing water and, at one time, fields of camas. Camas (*Camassia quamash*, or blue camas) is an attractive plant with a lovely blue or sometimes purple flower. It grows a nutritious root about the size and shape of a tulip bulb, prized by Indians wherever found, but especially throughout the Columbia Plateau and Snake River Plain. Generations of Bannock, Shoshone, Nez Perce, Flathead, and Pend d'Oreille assembled at Big Camas Prairie annually to harvest the roots, socialize, and trade salmon, pine nuts, bison hides, horses, buckskins, and other goods. This annual gathering was an important event in the social and economic calendar of the native people of the region.[232] Although camas was the most important food gathered here, several other roots such as yampa and *kuiyu* (tobacco root) and various seeds were also collected. It was here, too, that people met in preparation for the annual bison hunt on Montana's southern plains. The large horse herds fueled up on the rich grasslands at Big Camas Prairie to prepare for the long trip that often went through northern Yellowstone National Park. It was here that the Bannock Trail began (see Chapter 7).

Camas was gathered in late spring and early summer as the blooms began to die back. Roots were dug with sticks, then dried and stored for winter use. Without stores of camas, people would be ill prepared for the cold months of the year. The central role of roots like camas is reflected in the name "Digger," a label often assigned to unmounted native people in the Great Basin and surrounding regions.[233] The term was considered derogatory but was a clear reference to the common and important practice of digging roots for food. Agency reports routinely mention the departure of Shoshone, Bannock, Northern Paiute, and Nez Perce

Figure 28. Camas plant. (Redrawn from D. Statham 1982).

from the reservations for the "root grounds."[234] Some idea of the value of camas roots comes from ethnographer Julian Steward, who reported that one-half bushel of camas could be traded for a colt.[235]

So important was Camas Prairie as a source of food and a place for annual gatherings that the Bannock and probably the Northern Shoshone were at one time referred to as the "Great Kammas Indians" by the Secretary of the Interior and the "Great Kammas Prairie" was to be reserved as a summer home for them.[236] Bannock Chief Tahgee argued hard for the "Kamas Plains" to be included in their reservation in a council held on Long Tom Creek near Big Camas Prairie in 1867:

> I want the reservation large enough for all my people and no white men on it, except the Agent, other officers and employees of the Government. I want the right-of-way for my people to travel when on the way to and from the Buffalo Country, and when going to sell their furs and skins. I want the right to camp and dig roots on Camas prairie, when coming to Boise to trade. Some of my people have no horses; they could remain at Camas prairie while others went on to Boise.[237]

Chief Tahgee insisted that it be named in the Fort Bridger Treaty of 1868 as a part of the Shoshone-Bannock reservation:

> Article 2. It is agreed that whenever the Bannacks [sic] desire a reservation to be set apart for their use, or whenever the President of the United States shall deem it advisable for them to be put upon a reservation, he shall cause a suitable one to be selected for them in their present country, which shall embrace reasonable portions of the "Port Neuf" and *"Kansas Prairie"*[238] [sic] countries, and that, when this reservation is declared, the United States will secure to the Bannacks to same rights and privileges therein, and make the same and like expenditures therein for their benefit, except the agency-house and residence of agent, in proportion to their numbers, as herein provided for the Shoshonee reservation.

In 1877, during another gathering of Fort Hall Indians, Bannock leader Major Jim spoke eloquently of the importance of Camas Prairie and repeated the request to have the area part of the Fort Hall Reservation:

> Your people make farms and fence up all the country; the Indians make their farm too, which is the Great Camas Prairie, where our women dig roots to feed them and the children. The white men drive too many hogs and cattle upon the prairie, which eat up the roots of the Camas and destroy the plant. . . . When the Camas is destroyed[,] our children will suffer from hunger. . . . We do not like Fort Hall. It is too cold. Nothing will grow there. We wish to have the Great Camas Prairie put with

the Fort Hall Reservation, so that we can live there in summer and dig Camas. We never sold, or gave away Camas Prairie. We had nothing to do with any treaty which would take it away from us. . . . [239]

Apparently the failure of the government to assign Camas Prairie to the Fort Hall Reservation is at least in part due to the misspelling of the name in the Fort Bridger Treaty.

In the spring of 1878 southern Idaho settlers once drove herds of cattle, horses, and hogs onto Camas Prairie. In protest, Bannock Chief Buffalo Horn demanded that the livestock be removed from these gathering grounds. The settlers, recognizing the seriousness of the request, agreed. Before they could remove their livestock, two young Bannock men, one of them angered over gambling losses, seriously wounded two men, Lew Kensler and George Nesby. The Bannock War was on.

Although this incident and the intrusion of livestock onto the Camas gathering grounds appear to be the cause of the war (some referred to it as the "Camas Prairie War"), a number of events led up to the outbreak of hostilities.[240] Frustration with the failure of the federal government to meet treaty obligations, chronic food shortages, incessant pressure on Indian lands by white settlers, and the outbreak of the Nez Perce War of 1877 (see Chapter 5) all contributed to the Bannock War of 1878. The final chapters of that event played out in the newly established Yellowstone National Park.

Indian Frustrations

For a decade Fort Hall Indian agent W. H. Danilson drew attention to ongoing food shortages on the reservation, and the years leading up to the Bannock War were no exception. On April 20, 1876, for example, Danilson reports that he had run out of food, except for the families of about 300 farmers, laborers, sick, and elderly:

> The rations of more than a thousand Indians were thus cut off, and they were thrown upon their own resources for a living. This, too, in a season of the year when the mountains and foothills were covered with snow, and in a country where, under the most favorable circumstances, game is hard to obtain. Large numbers came to the office begging most piteously for food, stat-

Figure 29. Bannock Indians at Fort Hall, Idaho, in either 1872 or 1878. Buffalo Horn, one of the leaders during the Bannock War, is on a horse at the far left. (W. H. Jackson, photographer, Bureau of American Ethnology, Smithsonian Institution, Photo Archives, Brigham Young University, Neg. No. P80.)

ing that their children were crying for bread, which I well knew was the truth.[241]

About 250 Bannock were spending the winter on the plains of Montana that year or the situation would have been worse.

Other agents in the region faced similar circumstances partially due to the resolve of Congress to make Indians self-supporting. Agent W. V. Rinehart at the Malheur Agency in eastern Oregon found his annual appropriations cut from $50,000 in 1873 to $20,000 in 1877.[242] John A. Wright at the Lemhi Agency on the Salmon River in Idaho was likewise allocated $20,000 for his agency in 1878. He maintained this modest budget left him with 87¢ per person per week to supply all the necessities to run the agency including "goods, provisions . . . instructing Indians in agricultural and mechanical pursuits, in providing employees, educating children, procuring medicine, and medical attendance, care and support of the aged, sick, and infirm."[243] This figure dropped to 44¢ per Indian per week by 1879. Fortunately, not all the Indians assigned to that agency (which routinely included between 100 and 200 Bannock) stayed there for very long.[244]

These chronic shortages tested the patience of the Bannock at Fort Hall. They complained bitterly that supplies provided for their agency were being consumed by Shoshone, who should have been obtaining their provisions at the Wind River Reservation in Wyoming. Nonetheless, food rations were again scarce at the Fort Hall Agency during the winter of 1877–78. This was despite the fact that the main population of Bannock had spent the winter on the plains. As in past years, the food was gone by spring and the majority of the Indian population left the reservation, presumably for Camas Prairie, where their traditional food would soon be available.

After the 1877 Nez Perce flight through Idaho, tensions among settlers and Indian agents ran high. The Office of Indian Affairs feared that friends of the Nez Perce might decide to join in their military campaign. The fears seemed well grounded when, in August 1877, a young Bannock man, without apparent provocation, shot and wounded two Anglos. The event is detailed in a letter penned by Orson James, one of the wounded:

> Ross Fork Agency, August 8 '77
> Dear Sister : — I have a sad story to tell you. Today I lost some of my cattle and was going out to hunt them when an Indian rode up and shot me. The ball struck near the backbone and came out of my right side. The wound is not mortal, but it is bad enough. The Indian before shooting me shot a boy [Robert Boyd] that lives with and drives for John James, of Malad. The ball struck the left side of his neck and came out of his shoulder; the wound is very bad but not dangerous. [245]

The account of Indian agent W. H. Danilson, written only a week after the event, blames it on the Nez Perce uprising:

> I have to report a very serious affair which occurred here on the morning of the 7th instant. Robert Boyd and Orson James, both freighters, were shot by a young Bannock Indian, and severely wounded, the former in the neck and the latter in the

back—both flesh wounds. The men were immediately taken in charge by the agency physician, who has been untiring in his efforts for their comfort. At this writing they are both improving rapidly. The Bannocks had been rather restless for several days previous to this occurrence partly in consequence of the Nez Perce war, and partly because of a rumor that troops were coming to fight them. On the morning of the shooting a tramp came to the trading-post, stating he had been driven in by hostiles. The Indians, supposing that the Nez Perces were near the agency, made hurried preparations to go in pursuit. During the excitement a Bannock Indian shot the two teamsters as above mentioned. The headmen of both tribes denounced the shooting, and promised that the murderer should be arrested and severely punished.[246]

The Indian who shot James and Boyd was arrested and put in jail in Malad, Idaho, which angered the Bannock. During the ensuing tensions, the prisoner's brother, Tambiago, shot and killed Alex Rhoden, a thirty-year-old man who had assisted in delivering cattle to the reservation. The motives for shooting Rhoden were that he was a "notorious troublemaker who had publicly insulted [Tambiago] at the trading post at Fort Hall."[247] Tambiago fled but was eventually arrested in January 1878. Tambiago was hanged on June 28, 1878, after the Bannock War was under way. Just before his execution, Tambiago was asked why the Bannock had gone to war. His paraphrased response appeared on June 29, 1878, in *The Idaho Weekly Statesman*:

> [The war] was owing to the discontent of the Indians with their agent at Fort Hall, and with the *gray beard*—meaning the missionary—who had been sent there to teach them. . . . The Camas Prairie, he said, belonged of right to the Indians, and that they needed, but did not name this as one of the immediate causes of the outbreak.[248]

The dissatisfaction expressed for Agent Danilson stemmed in part from his apparent tendency to favor the Shoshone over the Bannock despite the fact that Fort Hall was originally a Bannock agency. In addition, Danilson kept about 600 head of his own cattle on the reservation.[249]

Shortly after Tambiago was arrested, the army, worried about additional hostilities, captured about 300 horses, assorted firearms, and 53 Bannock men. The men were returned to the reservation and, at Danilson's insistence, the horses and guns were also returned. He knew the Indians would need them if they were to survive the winter. Danilson also requested that the soldiers remain at Fort Hall to keep the peace. They were sent to Fort Douglas, Utah,[250] despite the general concern by Idaho settlers that hostilities were imminent. So great were their worries that, by January, several settlers had commenced constructing stockades.[251]

Onset of Conflict

By spring, tensions were high among Indians and settlers. On May 28, 1878, Idaho Territory governor Brayman wrote to Gen. O. O. Howard,

> The Indians claim Big Camas Prairie for hunting and collecting camas roots, and assemble there in large force each summer. White men, with large bands of cattle, and especially hogs are also pushing upon the same ground and disputes arise, endangering the peace.
>
> I do not think the Bannocks intend war, but do fear personal collusion and bloodshed, with their wide-spread consequences. The trial of the Indian who murdered Rhoden is now progressing at Malad City, Oneida Co. Should he be convicted, then executed, trouble may follow.[252]

The attack on Kensler and Nesby mentioned earlier occurred on May 30.

A general concern by the settlers in Idaho and Oregon was the possibility that Northern Paiute on the Malheur Reservation would join their Bannock kinsmen. When news of the hostilities reached them, the Paiute left the agency.[253] In addition, whites were concerned about Buffalo Horn, the somewhat opportunistic leader of the hostiles. He had some knowledge of military tactics and recent experience as a scout under Gen. O. O. Howard helping to round up the Nez Perce. As early as April, well before the confrontation at Big Camas Prairie, a Bannock party visited the Shoshone reservation at Elko, Nevada, and invited the Western Shoshone there to join them in an uprising.[254] This action is evidence of Bannock discontent with conditions on the reservation and supports the conclusion that the invasion of stock onto Big Camas Prairie was the last straw.

As expected, Buffalo Horn and about 150 warriors headed west from Big Camas Prairie to ask their Northern Paiute kinsmen to join them. Like the Bannock, the Northern Paiute were not happy with conditions on the reservation, nor did they care for Agent Rinehart. Neither Chief Winnemucca nor Egan, both leaders of the Malheur Paiute, wanted war. On June 8, in one of the early skirmishes of the war, Buffalo Horn was killed and his followers fled toward Steens Mountain in southeastern Oregon to meet up with the Paiute. It was clear that many of the Malheur people wanted war, including Oytes, an influential subchief and medicine man.[255] However, it was Egan who eventually assumed the leadership of the hostiles.[256] Now following the respected Chief Egan, the combined forces of Paiute and Bannock fled north, hopeful of recruiting Umatilla and Cayuse reinforcements. General Howard pursued the Indians who were terrorizing settlers along their route. The fleeing Indians stopped at the Columbia River.

The war turned against the Bannock and their allies when Chief Egan was killed by some Umatilla pretending to be interested in joining the Bannock cause. Approaching the Bannock camp the band of about forty Umatilla asked Egan and his leaders to leave the camp so they could privately explain the conditions under which they might be allowed to return to the reservation. Once away from the camp, the Umatilla seized Chief Egan with the intention of carrying him to the military camp. He resisted, and he and three of his warriors were killed.[257] Egan's death decimated the Indians and spelled the beginning of the end of the Bannock War. The renegades split into a number of smaller groups and were pursued by troops. Most of the Indians fled to join with friendlies on reservations. Others were killed during a series of small battles with the military.

By August, a raiding party had decided to make a run to Canada to join Sitting Bull, much like the Nez Perce the year before. They chose the Bannock Trail through Yellowstone and at Henry's Lake met up with the camp of a United States Geological Survey party under the direction of A. D. Wilson.[258] The Bannock succeeded in running off with the party's livestock and some provisions. The survey party was part of a larger group directed by Surveyor General Ferdinand Hayden, who reported the encounter between Wilson and the Bannock:

I have the honor to report that the division of the Survey with which I am connected arrived at the Upper Geyser Basin on the 26th of August. Soon after our arrival, Mr. A. D. Wilson, in charge of the Primary Triangulation, and party came into our camp on foot, having been robbed of their entire outfit, near Henry's Lake, on the evening of the 25th by a band of Bannock Indians.

Mr. Wilson had completed his station on the summit of Sawtelle's Peak and the party was in camp sitting around the campfire when the Indians fired into their camp, and at the same time ran off all their animals consisting of 12 mules and 2 horses. Mr. Wilson and party concealed themselves in the bushes until morning and then marched to our camp, a distance of about 60 miles. Fortunately, no one was hurt. Mr. Wilson in the night threw his great Theodolite and Barometer into the bushes, and Saturday he returned with them safely.[259]

The militia at Fort Ellis was on the alert due to news of other Bannock raids. A company of cavalry traveled up the Madison River and encountered a Bannock camp (most likely the same group who had run off Wilson's party) at Henry's Lake and captured their horse herd, but the Indians escaped into the Park.[260] The next week "all the livestock from Boetters ranche [sic] to Hot Springs" was stolen, probably by these same Bannock.

There were only a few tourists in the Park at the time, but Superintendent Norris, when he heard of the problems, decided to forge a "trail" from Mammoth to Upper Geyser Basin to allow military access through the Park. The road skirted the edge of Obsidian Cliffs, undoubtedly doing serious damage to the integrity of this important archaeological site, a fact that was certainly not a concern to Norris. His description of his efforts to cut a path for the road at the base of the cliff is worth quoting at length:

> Obsidian there rises like basalt in vertical columns many hundreds of feet high, and countless huge masses had fallen from this utterly impassable mountain into the hissing hot-spring margin of an equally impassable lake [Beaver Lake], without either Indian or game trail over the glistering [sic] fragments of nature's glass, sure to severely lacerate. As this glass barricade

sloped from some 200 or 300 feet high against the cliff at an angle of some 45 [degrees] to the lake, we—with the slivered fragments of timber thrown from the heights—with huge fires, heated and expanded, and then, men well screened by blankets held by others, by dashing cold water, suddenly cooled and fractured the large masses. Then with huge levers, steel bars, sledge, pick, and shovels, and severe laceration of at least the hands and faces of every member of the party, we rolled, slid, crushed, and shoveled one fourth of a mile of good wagon-road midway along the slope; it being, so far as I am aware, the only road of native glass upon the continent.[261]

This 60-mile-long wagon road, hacked out in less than a month, ended near the Middle Geyser Basin. Norris joined W. H. Holmes and the Hayden party just as Wilson and Park gamekeeper Harry Yount arrived on their flight from the Bannock. When informed by a scout who had just traveled the newly cut road of the fresh tracks of the hostile Bannock cutting across it, Norris, fearful of additional attacks, escorted the surveying party back to Mammoth. Here they were defended by the military with a Gatling gun.[262]

End of the War

Oddly, the main band of marauding Bannock was defeated by a group of tourists, albeit a very specialized group. Col. Nelson Miles, then commander at Fort Keogh, was headed to Yellowstone for a vacation with a group of fellow officers and their families (which, strictly speaking, made them tourists) when he heard of the proximity of the hostile Indians. Miles was accompanied by a detachment of soldiers and the 5th Infantry band. They reached the Crow Agency on August 29, heard of the Bannock presence, and sent a detachment to find them. Lieutenant Clark of the 2nd Cavalry first encountered the Indians near Index Peak on the eastern border of the Park. On September 4, Miles surprised the Bannock camp on the Clarks Fork near Heart Mountain, killing 11 and capturing 31 along with 200 horses and mules.[263]

On September 12, another segment of Bannock, escapees from the Clarks Fork confrontation, met up with Lt. Hoel Bishop of the 5th Cavalry on Dry Fork, a tributary of the Snake River southwest of

Yellowstone Lake. Bishop was accompanied by thirty soldiers and 150 Shoshone from the Wind River Reservation. After a brief struggle, the Indians gave up the battle. The army reported "one Indian killed; five women, a boy, a girl, and eleven horses and three mules . . . captured." The incident is described in more graphic terms by Thomas LeForge:

> The Bannock decided to surrender to the troops, and they moved in a peaceful manner to do so. Nevertheless, volleys of gun-fire were poured into them and several of them were killed. I remember that one woman had a thigh broken by a bullet. She hid out with her baby, but she was discovered, brought in to the agency, and cared for until her recovery. It seemed to me that killing these Indians when it was plainly evident they were trying to surrender was a violation of the humanities. They did not respond to the fire.[264]

The captives maintained that twenty-eight had died on Clarks Fork and admitted to having stolen livestock from the Hayden Yellowstone party.

Yellowstone historian Richard Bartlett notes that the Bannock War ended Indian presence in Yellowstone, except for some continued hunting by small groups of Bannock and Shoshone in the south and southwest portions of the Park.[265] However, Park personnel had no way of knowing that conflict was at an end. Preparations to deal with Indian problems continued, although unnecessarily.

Retrospect

Today a visitor to Big Camas Prairie would be hard pressed to find camas except in roadside borrow pits.[266] Scenes of Indian camps scattered across the grassy plain, large, restless horse herds, children racing, campfires burning into the night, and the hypnotic chants of gambling songs may seem remote, even fantastic to today's residents, but in the not too distant past such scenes were an annual occurrence. Few realize that it was here that the tragic Bannock War began and fewer still recognize that the events of that conflict marked the end of Bannock-Shoshoni band organization.[267] Certainly, that war also dropped the final curtain on the use of the Bannock Trail that had traditionally had its start here on the camas gathering grounds.

7

The Bannock Trail

In the northern portion of Yellowstone Park, between Indian Creek and the Lamar River, remnants of the Great Bannock Trail are still clearly visible to those who know how and where to look. This trail was named for the Bannock Indians, who were perhaps its primary travelers. It came to be an important route for all groups of mounted Idaho Indians who depended heavily on the pursuit of the bison for food, clothing, and other domestic items. Fort Hall and Lemhi Shoshone, Nez Perce, and Flathead all used the trail separately and sometimes together.

This route through Yellowstone was likely used throughout much of prehistory, but it experienced greatly increased travel during the mid-1800s. The reasons for this are historical. Prior to about 1840 bison were relatively abundant on the Snake River Valley and the northern Great Basin. In 1841, Osborne Russell commented on the drastic change in the availability of big game in this region:

> In the year 1836 large bands of buffalo could be seen in almost every little valley on the small branches of this stream; at this time the only traces which could be seen of them were the scattered bones of those that had been killed. Their trails which had been made in former years, deeply indented in the earth, were overgrown with grass and weeds. The trappers often remarked to each other as they rode over these lonely plains that it was time for the white man to leave the mountains as beaver and game had nearly disappeared.[268]

It is clear that at one time bison were plentiful. In 1834 William Ferris stated that they were "numerous at the forks of the Henry's Fork and Snake River."[269] Later that same year observing bison on the Snake River Plain, he wrote, "We saw immense herds of buffalo in the plains below, which were covered in every direction by them, as far as the eye could

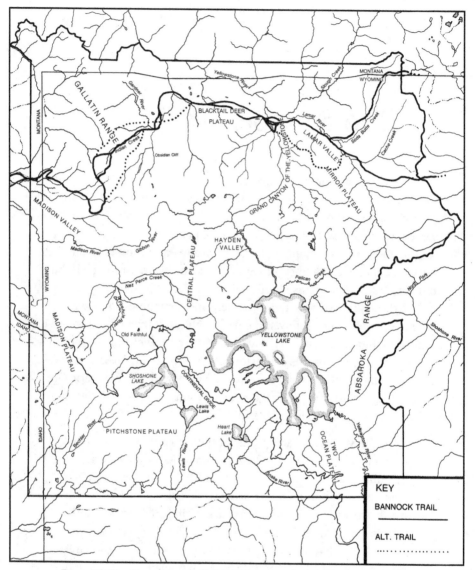

Figure 30. The Great Bannock Trail in Yellowstone Park. [After Replogle 1956.]

distinguish."[270] Russell's comments are similar. During the summer of 1835 on the Snake River plain west of present-day Idaho Falls, he observed, "I lay all day and watched the Buffaloe which were feeding in immense bands all about me." The next day, "The Buffaloe were carelessly feeding all over the plain as far as the eye could reach."[271]

Ferris's map notation states that before 1835 bison roamed west of Fort Hall, but after that time they "are annually returning eastward whence they came." This comment is a little enigmatic since it suggests the movement of bison onto the Snake River from the east is a singular, perhaps even a historic, event, and interpretations must remain inconclusive.

The disappearance of the bison from the Snake River Plain and perhaps northern Utah seems quite rapid given the large numbers once present. Karen Lupo suggests that both ecological (massive snowstorms in the region in 1836) and cultural (over-hunting) factors account for the depletion.[272] The latter seems more reasonable given Russell's documentation of excessive hunting pressure pushing the bison back across the continental divide into the headwaters of the Missouri.[273] Some idea of the number of bison being taken by the Indians comes from Russell watching the Bannock killing "upwards of a Thousand cows"[274] in a single day. If accurate, this kind of slaughter suggests that Steward was correct in concluding that the twin hunting tools of horses and firearms by the Indians and increased hunting by trappers were the primary reasons for the demise of bison.[275]

Regardless, once the bison were gone, Indian groups west of the Rockies who had adapted the Plains lifestyle preferred risking retaliation from the Blackfeet and Crow for hunting in enemy territory to returning to their former lifeway. Warm robes, spacious tipis, and hundreds of pounds of meat were more attractive than the rabbit-skin robes, brush wickiups, and seeds used a century before.

Trail Routes

Undoubtedly the Bannock Trail was only one of many routes used by prehistoric man to cross the Rockies. Early Park historian Hiram Chittenden commented, "Indian trails, though generally indistinct, were everywhere found inside the Park by the early explorers, generally on lines since occupied by the tourist routes."[276] He described a primary trail running north to south following the Yellowstone River Valley to Yellowstone Lake, where it divided. One branch followed the east shore and the modern Thorofare Trail over Two Ocean Pass and thence southward, until it joined other trails. The west shore trail crossed into the Grand Tetons, Jackson Lake, and the Snake River drainage. Other important trails also followed the major rivers—the Madison and Firehole.[277]

The easiest way for the Bannock and others to move from the Pacific to the Atlantic drainage and to access bison country was to simply drop over the barely perceptible continental divide at Raynold's Pass. The pass separates Henry's Lake from the Madison and Three Forks river valley hunting grounds. Significantly, Three Forks was within the territory claimed by the Blackfeet, historical enemies of the Bannock and Shoshone. Relatively easy routes over the mountains also lay east and southeast, but these led into ranges already depleted by the Eastern Shoshone, the Ute, and trappers. The remaining route lay north and east across the Park and friendly Sheepeater country onto the rich hunting grounds of Montana. Part of the appeal of the Bannock Trail was the strategic advantage it offered. As it cut across the northern portion of the Park, the trail accessed a series of river valleys that were potential avenues to the bison prairies. While the main camp waited in the safety of the mountains, fast-moving scouts could be dispatched down the rivers (for example, the Madison, Gallatin, Yellowstone, or Clarks Fork) to check for the presence of enemy camps and locate game.

The Bannock Trail began near Camas Meadows in south central Idaho. It followed the Snake River east and north, eventually ascended Henry's Fork of the Snake River, and entered the Yellowstone region via Henry's Lake Flats and Targhee Pass. Near Horse Butte, a few miles north of West Yellowstone in the upper Madison Valley, the Bannock Trail was joined by branch trails from the Madison and Gallatin Valleys. Great Springs, now Corey Springs, was a popular camp just west of the Park boundary on the shore of modern Hebgen Lake.[278] From here the main trail entered present-day Yellowstone Park along the Duck Creek drainage toward the head of Cougar Creek and then cut north to cross the Gallatin Range just west of Mount Holmes at an elevation of 9,300 feet. The trail then descended Indian Creek to its juncture with the Gardner River, and turned across Swan Lake flats and over Snow Pass to Mammoth. Here it was joined by other minor trails coming up the Yellowstone drainage. N. P. Langford, the chronicler of the 1870 Washburn Expedition, describes the trail and its several routes in this area:

> There are seemingly two trails across the mountain—a cir-
> cuitous one by as easy a grade as can be found, over which the

Figure 31. Ranger Wayne Replogle on the Bannock Trail near Blacktail, 1955. (D. Condon, photographer, YNP Photo Archives, Neg. No. YELL 37838-1.)

Indians send their families with their heavily laden pack horses;
and a more direct, though more difficult, route which the war
parties use in making their rapid rides.

The trail stayed generally south of the Yellowstone River as it crossed
the Gardner River, Lava Creek, and Blacktail Deer Creek. After fording
the Yellowstone River near Tower Falls, the trail followed the Lamar
River to its juncture with Soda Butte Creek, where the trail split. One
track followed a more circuitous route to the Clarks Fork along Soda
Butte Creek; another left the Lamar River and struck directly over the
divide into the Clarks Fork drainage. Assorted side routes, minor trails,
and the main trail combined to form a system of travel through Yellowstone that varied with such factors as weather and the presence of enemies and game.

The trail led ultimately to a favorite hunting ground of many of the western tribes—including the Nez Perce, Kalispel, Kutenai, Pend d'Oreille, Flathead, and Shoshone—between the Yellowstone and Musselshell Rivers in Montana. The Shoshone called it *Kutsunambihi,* "the buffalo heart," after a heart-shaped rock formation located about 40 miles northwest of Billings. The area was between traditional territories of the Crow and Blackfoot, and was claimed by both. The effect was that the region was somewhat neutral.[279]

The Bannock Trail, 1838–1878

The Park had been traversed by man for centuries, but the extermination of the bison in the Basin-Plateau region resulted in a surge of traffic along this thoroughfare between 1838 and 1878. Haines described the use of the Bannock trail over this period in three phases. The first, 1838–1862, were the "golden years" when the Bannock traveled freely to the bison grounds. No treaties bound them, no settlers yet intruded upon their homeland, and Yellowstone was still "undiscovered." The second phase, 1862–1868, was a time of transition from the traditional patterns of unfettered movement to settling on the Fort Hall Reservation. The reservation was formed as a consequence of numerous factors including the 1863 Battle of Bear River, where General Conner massacred a large group of Shoshone and some Bannock. In this period the Bannock had to reroute the trail south over the rugged Absaroka Mountains to avoid the developing mines in the Cooke City area. During the third phase, 1868–1878, the Bannock were being pressured by the reservation agent to settle down, but, without the annual trek to obtain bison, they were faced with starvation. A critical event at this time was the death of Chief Targhee in the winter of 1870–71. Unfortunately, no comparable leader arose to replace him. Due to conflicts with the other struggling tribes—Sioux, Nez Perce, Arapahoe, and Crow—and finally skirmishes with the whites, the Bannock were asked to give up their homes and guns, a request that led to the Bannock War of 1878 (see Chapter 7).

Modern highways through the Park follow closely the Bannock Trail and other prehistoric paths trod for centuries by Native Americans.[280]

8

Indians
and Yellowstone Geysers

Historians' opinions differ regarding the attitude of native peoples toward the geysers and hot springs of Yellowstone Park. Early reporters and explorers especially stated unequivocally that the Indians feared the thermal features and avoided the Park. P. W. Norris, Park superintendent from 1877 to 1882, took this stand in his 1878 report to the Secretary of the Interior:

> Owing to the isolation of the park deep amid snowy mountains, and the superstitious awe of the roaring cataracts, sulphur pools, and spouting geysers over the surrounding pagan Indians, they seldom visit it, and only a few harmless Sheep-eater hermits, armed with bows and arrows, ever resided there, and even they are now vanished.[281]

This idea, perpetuated by various guidebooks and histories, continued well into the twentieth century. Recall the quote from Stoddard's Lectures that stated, "The region of the Yellowstone was to most Indian tribes a place of horror. They trembled at the awful sights they here beheld" (see note 11). Wingate's account of his 1885 trip through Yellowstone included his speculation that, "it is probable that their (Indians') superstitious awe of the spouting geysers prevented them from frequently visiting it themselves."[282] A 1913 copy of *Campbell's Guide* diminished Native American use and knowledge of the Park, which was probably intended to calm visitors' fears of Indian presence:

> That all these tribes crossed the present borders of the Park is evidenced by their trails, but these trails were little used, and

Figure 32. Eruption of Giant Geyser in Yellowstone Park. (Photographer unknown, Photo Archives, Brigham Young University, Neg. No. P167.)

probably never used except in cases of necessity. . . . The Indians knew little of the Park and said less; it was to them a region of burning mountains to be let severely alone, and the few that probably did see the geysers and boiling lakes told the others about it and they were willing to take their word for it and didn't take any chances that, to them, seemed to be so devoid of the presence of the Great Spirit.[283]

Campbell was especially ethnocentric in his descriptions of the American Indian, and comments on the abundance of trails in the Park managed to slip in one about geysers and Indians:

The earlier explorers of the Park found trails, evidently Indian, running north and south, east and west, but on routes, studiously avoiding any locality suggesting a geyser.[284]

More recently, Yellowstone historians maintained that Indians were not afraid of the geysers at all. A member of this group is Yellowstone Park historian Merrill Beal, who expressed,

While it is true that superstition and taboo loomed large in primitive experience there is no reason to suppose that Indians gave Wonderland a wide berth. Rather there is an abundance of material evidence that controverts this view. Furthermore, the proposition is at once illogical and untrue historically.[285]

Perhaps the most recent well-researched position Joseph Weixelman's. He argues strongly that Indians were not afraid of the Yellowstone geysers; rather, he states, "Euro-Americans originated this idea and it must be dispelled before we can understand the true nature of Yellowstone's human past."[286]

Evidence for Indian Responses to Yellowstone

The evidence falls into two categories: ethnohistoric/ethnographic and archaeological. The former includes the observations of early explorers about Indian behavior toward thermal actions and interviews with various Indians regarding their beliefs about the geysers and hot springs. The latter depends on the presence of material items that accumulate in the areas where early people spent time camping or hunting.

While examining the evidence, it is important to consider specific details regarding the points critical to the issue. First of all, did Indians avoid the entire Yellowstone region or just a portion of it? Second, which geological features were the Indians afraid of—all of them, including the quiet hot pools, the mud pots, the geysers, and even the cataracts? Finally, who were the Indians who were supposed to have avoided these features? The Sheepeaters, the only relatively permanent Park inhabitants? Or the groups who occasionally traveled through Yellowstone on their trading and hunting trips? The following section considers these varying questions.

Ethnohistoric / Ethnographic

The earliest report of Indian response to the geysers comes from W. A. Ferris, who visited the Upper Geyser Basin in 1834. With him were two Pend d'Oreille Indians who spoke a language related to, and who lived near, the Salish-speaking Flatheads of western Montana. Ferris approached one of the basins and tested the waters:

I ventured near enough to put my hand into the water of its basin, but withdrew it instantly, for the heat of the water . . . was altogether too great for comfort, and the agitation of the water, the disagreeable effluvium continually exuding, and the hollow unearthly rumbling under the rock on which I stood, so ill accorded with my notions of personal safety, that I retreated back precipitately to a respectful distance. The Indians who were with me, were quite appalled, and could not by any means be induced to approach them [the geysers]. They seemed astonished at my presumption in advancing up to the large one, and when I safely returned, congratulated me on my "narrow escape." They believed them to be supernatural [and] supposed them to be the production of the Evil Spirit.[287]

Another early record comes from Father DeSmet's travel journal, about 1850:

The Indians pass these places [the geysers] in profound silence and with superstitious dread. They regard them as the abode of underground spirits always at war with one another, and continually at the anvil forging their weapons. They never pass without leaving some offering on a conspicuous point of the mysterious region.[288]

However, since DeSmet did not personally visit Yellowstone, these impressions are secondhand and are not specific to the Indian groups affected.

Osborne Russell encountered the Blackfeet on Pelican Creek near Yellowstone Lake in 1839 but did not observe their reactions to the geysers. Some 25 years later the Blackfeet told Father Francis Xavier Kuppens of the wonders of Yellowstone and eventually took him to Yellowstone Falls (lower falls), Yellowstone Lake, and the geysers in 1865.[289] These two reports suggest the Blackfeet were familiar with the Park and its wondrous features. Lt. Gustavus Doane and N. P. Langford both related encounters with the Crow near Tower Falls during their visit to the Park with the Washburn party in 1870. Probably based on his communication with the Crows at this time, Doane said that "the larger tribes" did not enter the geyser basins on account of "superstitious ideas in connection with thermal springs."[290]

Supt. P. W. Norris's reports contain many references to Indian relics in the Park and the attitude of the Indians regarding the hot springs and geysers. Apparently he discussed this very topic with them. He quotes a Wind River Shoshone, Wesaw:

> He said that his people [Shoshones], the Bannocks, and Crows occasionally visited the Yellowstone Lake and River portions of the Park, but very seldom the geyser regions which he declared were "heap heap bad," and never wintered there, as white men sometimes did with horses.[291]

In 1882 Yellowstone was visited by Gen. Philip Sheridan, who was guided by five Sheepeaters from the mountains south of Yellowstone Lake. Sheridan reports that these Indians had never visited the geyser basins and exhibited more astonishment and wonder at them than any of his group. He attributes their previous avoidance of the geysers to superstition. Another late-nineteenth-century report comes from Finn Burnett, a pioneer resident at the Wind River Reservation, who states that the Indians (probably the Wind River Shoshone) were much afraid of the geysers and never visited them.[292] Gen. William T. Sherman, who visited Yellowstone just before the Nez Perce "invasion" in 1877, was convinced that the Indians would not enter the Park as it was "to their superstitious minds associated with hell by reason of its geysers and hot-springs."[293]

Contrasting with these reports are those offered by noted ethnographer Ake Hultkrantz, who studied the Plains or Wind River Shoshone in 1948. His informants stated that, indeed, the Shoshone believed the geysers contained spirits and prayed to them, and some avoided or hurried past the geysers on their visits.[294] Others, although frightened at first by the "steaming waters," discovered it was just water. They then undressed and bathed in the waters that went "up and down." The bathing may have been in part to enhance the bather's "medicine" or "spiritual power" or simply to feel better.[295]

Another of Hultkrantz's Shoshone informants told of his grandfather, Tavonasia, who was for a time a member of a Sheepeater band that spent summers in Yellowstone. The Tavonasia band, as they were called, camped near the geysers in the Firehole Basin, bathed in them, and prayed to their spirits. However, this informant stated emphatically that of all the warriors of Washakie's band only the Tavonasia band hunted there.[296]

Figure 33. Hot pool at the summit of Jupiter Terrace, Yellowstone Park. [Photograph by Gifford, Photo Archives, Brigham Young University, Neg. No. P384.]

In 1935 two veterans of the 1877 Nez Perce War, Many Wounds and White Hawk, revisited the Park. Asked about fear of the geysers and hot springs, they said that they were not afraid and implied that the Nez Perce, during their earlier visits to the Park, took advantage of the hot water by using it for cooking. They also stated,

> We know that Park country, no difference what white people say ! . . . We knew that country well before passing through there in 1877. The hot smoking springs and the high-shooting water were nothing new to us.[297]

In weighing this line of evidence against the questions stated above, it seems apparent that for the most part the neighboring or local Indians were not strangers to the Yellowstone region, and almost all were aware of the more spectacular thermal features in the major geyser basins. As to whether the Indians were more afraid of the hot springs or of the geysers, the evidence is not clear, but it does suggest that the active geysers, which were seen as containing spirits, were more likely to inspire awe. With respect to the final question—"Who were the Indians that were afraid of the thermal features?"—it seems that the locals were less apprehensive about the geysers than occasional visitors were. However, as we have seen, the reactions varied from individual to individual.

Archaeological Data

The archaeological evidence is much less controversial. In 1880 Norris reported that decaying lodges, which he attributed to the Sheepeaters, were "abundant near Mammoth Hot Springs, the various firehole basins, the shores of Yellowstone Lake, the newly explored Hoodoo Region, and in nearly all of the sheltered glens and valleys of the Park."[298] Norris's 1881 report also contains many references to driveways and miscellaneous artifacts collected in Yellowstone, although he does not mention their provenance.[299]

Archaeological reconnaissance work by the University of Montana in the late 1950s and early 1960s, combined with earlier work, identified nearly 500 pre-European archaeological sites in Yellowstone,[300] including the Norris Geyser and the Lower and Upper Geyser basins. The majority of these archaeological finds date earlier than the historic period and assigning any to Shoshone-speaking Sheepeaters, who arrived in the vicinity probably as recently as the 1800s, is problematic (see Chapter 2 for more on this topic).

Falling somewhere in between archaeological and historic evidences are the Bannock and other Native American trails discussed in the last chapter. Although the Bannock Trail stayed north of the major geyser basins, it passed fairly close to Mammoth and the numerous steaming pools there. Haines reported numerous additional Indian trails, including one close to the geyser basins, near Yellowstone Lake and the West Thumb and the West Thumb Geyser Basin.[301]

Discussion

Archaeological, ethnohistoric, and ethnographic evidence suggests that Indians did not avoid geological oddities such as geysers. It is possible that certain groups or individuals avoided the more active thermal features, as might be predicted in light of what is known about the beliefs of Plains and the Great Basin Indians. Warriors of the Plains tribes, including the Shoshone, sought success in war and hunting through a quest for the power of various spirits via visions and dreams and went to places, such as mountains, known to be the haunts of spirits to obtain that power.[302] As a result, the geysers, while being held in awe by most and avoided by some, may have actually acted as a magnet for the ambitious. Steward found that the Lemhi Shoshone knew of a "hot spring near Yellowstone . . . favored [for the pursuit of power] but [which] was dangerous because of proximity of Blackfoot."[303] The various responses to the geysers by different Indians within the same group can be explained in part by the highly individualized nature of both Plains and Great Basin societies, and the lack of a uniform or highly structured belief system. The simplistic generalization that all Indians were afraid of the unique geological phenomena in Yellowstone also fits with preconceived notions about "primitive" groups and their propensity to attribute the strange or unusual to the supernatural.

Indigenous peoples within the Great Basin culture area, which includes Shoshone and Bannock, widely believed in water sprites or babies that dwelled in springs, lakes, or rivers.[304] These creatures often had malevolent intent, as they would creep into villages at night and steal unguarded babies or pull people into the water.[305] The Lemhi Shoshone called the water baby *Pau'ona*. It "has long hair, lives in the water and is mean and dangerous. If a baby is left alone in the brush, *Pau'ona* may kill and eat it."[306] Steward also found that Shoshone believe in the power of the "mountain dwarf," *Nunumbi*, and some sought after that power, especially for help in hunting.[307] The Lemhi Shoshone described *Nunumbi* as "a being that lives in the mountains, is friendly, looks and cries like a baby, is dressed like a man, carries a bow and arrows with eagle feathers, and can climb any place and kill eagles."[308] The baby-like crying is reminiscent of water babies mentioned above. These spirits held tremendous power, but it was a power that could work for or against an individual at the spirit's whim.[309] Although many feared this power, some sought it for success in hunting or shamanistic practices. Great Basin ethnographies do not specifically mention that water babies or other threatening spirits were connected to geysers.

Weixelman concludes that many native peoples, including Shoshone and Bannock, saw Yellowstone as sacred—a place to pursue visions. He draws attention to the possibility that it may have been (and be) difficult for Anglos to see the difference between expressions of reverence for sacred places and fear.[310] Weixelman concludes that "the thermal wonders of the Park did not frighten the native peoples of the region."[311] He uses the term "frighten" to counter the notion that Indians were afraid of the unknown in some child-like sense. Steward's research among the Northern Shoshone and Bannock reinforces this conclusion that a place like Yellowstone may have been a logical choice to pursue shamanistic or hunting power, as it is mountainous and, therefore, could be thought of as sacred.[312] However, hot (or cold) springs were clearly feared as possible abodes of water babies. When combined with the commonsense fear of hot water, Weixelman's statement is perhaps too sweeping. Fear of Park thermal features was not the same as a child's fear, but based in strongly held beliefs and/or a concern for personal safety.[313]

Merrill Beal explains Superintendent Norris's endorsement of the Indians' "fear" of Yellowstone as "an adaptation of business psychology to a promising national resort."[314] In other words, Norris chose to reassure potential tourists, who might fear the danger of Indian attack after the Nez Perce War and the attack on the Radersburg group, by maintaining that Yellowstone was avoided by all Indians.

9

The Jackson Hole War

The events of 1877, 1878, and 1879 did little to calm fears of Park administrators about Indian problems. One year after the Bannock War of 1878, Superintendent Norris built an administrative "fortress" atop Capitol Hill at Mammoth to more easily withstand Indian attacks.[315] This headquarters building included "an octagon turret or gun-room, 9 feet in diameter and 10 feet high, well-loop-holed for rifles"[316] He also constructed a blockhouse with rifle loopholes in Upper Geyser Basin. None of these defensive buildings were ever used to fend off Indian attacks, and the Capitol Hill Headquarters was torn down in 1909.[317] In 1879, the army assumed a presence in the Park region with a summer camp at Henry's Lake to keep Indian problems to a minimum.[318]

Sentiments expressed in an early guidebook assured tourists that the Indian threat was no more:

> In 1879, there were no Indian raids, but the Sheep-eaters, with a few raiding bands of Bannocks and Shoshones, made the possession of animals in the Park rather uncertain, although they killed no white man. Since that time the Indian difficulty has been cured, the Indians have been forced back on their distant reservations, and the traveler in the Park will see or hear no more of them than if he was in the Adirondacks or White Mountains.[319]

Although Yellowstone Park was never again threatened by Indian-related hostilities, problems for and with Indians continued.

The greater Yellowstone region, including Jackson Hole, was renowned for herds of large game animals—majestic elk and bison, deer, antelope, and mountain sheep—and for its wonderful fisheries. These plentiful resources enticed both Indian and white hunters, and the battle to preserve this natural bounty began with the Park's inception in

1872. In the 1880s and 1890s protecting game animals became a significant, and national, issue. Aubrey Haines referred to the 1880s as a time of the "Yellowstone Crusade," a conservation effort to preserve "game animals," the equivalent of grazers such as elk, deer, and bison (predators could be killed with impunity), and concluded in May 1894 with the passage of the Lacey Act. This act specifically prohibited the "hunting, or the killing or wounding, or capturing at any time of any bird or wild animal, except dangerous animals, when it is necessary to prevent them from destroying human life."[320] It also restricted fishing with seines, traps, and drugs.

The activities leading up to the Lacey Act effectively restricted Indian hunters from the lands south of the Park. Bannock from Fort Hall, Idaho, traditionally hunted the mountainous regions of Yellowstone and Grand Teton to supplement often meager rations on the reservation. In 1886 ranchers on the Montana-Idaho border next to Yellowstone complained to the Fort Hall agent about Indians burning grass to drive game to waiting hunters. Capt. Moses Harris, the first military superintendent of Yellowstone, immediately took up the cry of the Yellowstone Crusade by focusing on Indian poaching. In 1888 he complained to both the Lemhi and Fort Hall agencies about Indian hunting in and adjacent to the Park, referring to the "annoyance occasioned in previous years by the hunting operations in the vicinity of this National Park of Parties of Bannock Indians from the Fort Hall and Lemhi Agencies."[321] Not only were the Indians poaching, they "gave rise to much alarm and uneasiness among the tourist visitors" and tended to set fire to the grasslands and forests.[322] Harris failed to get satisfaction, so he penned a rather sarcastic and lengthy report to the Secretary of the Interior. He laid out his case of abuse by Bannock and Shoshone, supported by affidavits of reports of Indians hunting in and near the Park. Written testimony was provided by several individuals who had seen Bannock and Shoshone Indians between 1887 and 1889, mostly outside the Park near the southern boundary, but also near the western periphery near the headwaters of the Gallatin. In addition, two Bannock, a man and a woman, were seen near the Grand Canyon of the Yellowstone. In most cases, the Indians had had successful hunts and were described as supplied with "large quantities of dried meat and hides."[323] In two instances, forest fires were reported near the Indian camps. The Bannock couple near the Grand Canyon apparently had no meat with them.

Harris considered native use of Yellowstone's game as "unmitigated evil,"[324] hence his intense letter to curb the abuses. His appeal to local agents for support and assistance went largely unheeded for at least two reasons: The agents were keenly aware of the near-starved condition of their wards and they knew the Indians had been granted the right to hunt on unoccupied lands by the Fort Bridger Treaty of 1868. Harris seemed to be unaware of this, although he accused the Indians of "having no knowledge of the law."[325] Article 4 of the treaty states,

> The Indians herein named agree, when the agency house and other buildings shall be constructed on their reservations named, they will make said reservations their permanent home, and they will make no permanent settlement elsewhere; but they shall have the right to hunt on the unoccupied lands of the United States so long as game may be found thereon, and so long as peace subsists among the whites and Indians on the borders of the hunting districts.[326]

The conditions of this federal treaty were clearly in conflict with Wyoming's hunting seasons and limits, which did not allow hunting year-round. There was no mention in the treaty of observing local game laws that were established by states without consideration for the promises in the treaty.

In 1889 the complaints were addressed by the prestigious Boone and Crockett Club of New York City. Indians were accused of killing game for the hides only and hunting out of season. As a result, the Commissioner of Indian Affairs issued a letter to all agencies around Yellowstone (Fort Hall, Lemhi, Wind River, and Crow) that prohibited taking of game without using the meat. Further, if Indians hunted without proper permits, they would be restricted to their reservations.[327] Fort Hall agent J. T. Van Orsdale replied by pointing out that the Indians had been given the right to hunt on federal lands. He also noted the practice of guides in Jackson Hole who allowed their dude hunters from back east and foreign countries to hunt for horns only, or for the ivory eye teeth sought by members of the Benevolent Paternal Order of the Elks.[328] In addition, the agents knew the elk were an important source of cash for the Indians who manufactured gloves, moccasins, and other items for sale from the hides. The Jackson Hole accusers included a number of guides, twenty-five of whom made a living directing tourists to hunt big game.[329]

The Indian agent for the Shoshone Agency reported that "hordes of white hunters infested the country entirely unmolested."[330] Moses Harris was aware of hunting by non-Indians along the Park boundary. He stated, "The overflow of the Park game into the adjacent regions renders the vicinity of the Park a favorite hunting ground, not only for these Indians, but for gentlemen sportsmen from all parts of the world."[331] In 1895 acting superintendent Capt. George Anderson received funds to pursue white poachers who were killing bison near Henry's Lake, Idaho, presumably for "buffalo scalps" to sell in Butte. One group of poachers was nearly caught but escaped under cover of darkness. These activities were in violation of the newly passed Lacey Act and were apparently perpetrated by whites, since the reports do not mention Indians.[332]

In 1893 the dispute grew more heated and was a major issue in the 1894 election in Jackson Hole. Emotions came to a head in 1895 amidst problems with Van Orsdale's successor, Thomas B. Teter. Wyoming governor William A. Richards believed that more stringent measures were needed to curb the slaughter of elk and, thinking the conditions of the 1868 treaty were no longer in force, issued a directive that gave the Jackson Hole settlers his full support. Among other things, Richards wanted to "put the Indians out of Jackson Hole, and keep them out at all costs."[333] Officials of Marysvale, Wyoming, sent Constable William Manning with a posse of deputies to take care of the matter. In several separate incidents that summer, Manning found Bannock hunters with green hides and either arrested, fined, or imprisoned them. He did not win all the time. In June 1895, Manning, found fifteen Bannock with 40 elk hides and attempted to arrest them and transport them to Marysvale. The Bannock told the posse to "go to hell as they were not afraid [of the soldiers]," and Manning and his men backed off.[334] One Bannock party was arrested and imprisoned, only to be allowed to escape when it was clear they could not pay the $1,400 fine.[335]

In July 1895, Governor Richards contacted the Office of Indian Affairs and informed it that an Indian had been killed in an attempt to escape from Manning and his posse.[336]

On July 13, Constable Manning and a twenty-six-man posse encountered a Bannock camp of ten men, thirteen women, and a number of children on the Fall River. The posse waited through the night and surprised the Indians at daybreak, confiscating their arms, meat, packs, ration checks, and other goods. The posse arrested the Bannock and began a march to Marysvale. While en route, the Indians were told that they would be hanged or jailed once they reached town. Believing this, and seeing their captors loading their weapons as they were passing through a belt of timber, the Bannock panicked and tried to escape. The posse opened fire, killed an old man named Timega, wounded six others, and seriously wounded a young boy named Nemits. Two infants were lost in the confusion. Timega was shot in the back and lay dead in the woods for twenty days before his body was found and recovered. Nemits, shot through the back and with a bullet in his left arm, lived on dried meat for seventeen days and finally reached a ranch owned by an Indian sympathizer.[337] One of the infants survived and was carried to Fort Washakie where it was cared for by a Mormon family; the other was never found.

Each of these incidents was reported in the press and resulted in spiraling rumors of a new Bannock War, complete with the killing of settlers, burning of houses, and people fleeing for their lives. Headlines in the *Idaho Statesman* referred to "Marauding Bannocks" and a "Country Full of Indians." Others reported that the Bannock were on the warpath and that settlers had been killed and their homes burned.[338] The incident alarmed Yellowstone tourists, who quickly left the Park on the Northern Pacific Railroad.[339] Governor Richards telegraphed the Commissioner of Indian Affairs that "200 Indians supposed to be Utes were seen yesterday near South Pass, Fremont County; also 47 Sioux on Bad Water Creek . . . mounted, armed and without women or children."[340] All of this was greatly exaggerated; no Utes or Sioux were in the vicinity and there was no burning of settlers' homes. Fort Hall agent Thomas Teter's prompt investigation revealed that no settlers had been attacked, but he advised sending troops, as several hundred Indians had collected near Fall River, Idaho, and the possibility of conflict with settlers was real. Fortunately, Teter was able to convince the Bannock to return to Fort Hall before troops arrived or serious trouble erupted.[341]

Troops were dispatched to the Fort Hall reservation to control Indians unhappy about the actions of the posse that fired on the Indian hunters. No action was taken against Constable Manning and his men. The Indians sought the return of their equipment and eventually were allowed to recover seven rifles, twenty saddles, twenty blankets, one horse, nine packs of meat, and nine tepees, more or less.[342] The Manning attack was summed up by a U.S. District Attorney:

The whole affair was, I believe, a premeditated and prearranged plan to kill some Indians and thus stir up sufficient trouble to subsequently get United States troops into the region and ultimately have the Indians shut out from Jacksons Hole. The plan was successfully carried out and the desired results obtained.[343]

The same district attorney took a trip through the Jackson Hole area to determine the extent of damage to game animals by Indians.

During my stay in Jacksons Hole I visited many portions of the district and saw no evidences of such slaughter. . . . No carcasses or remains of elk were found in quantities to justify such charges. On August 12 I visited a camp of Bannock Indians who had been on a hunting trip in Jacksons Hole until ordered by the troops to return to their reservation. I found the Indian women of the party preparing the meat of seven or eight elk for winter use, drying and "jerking" it. Every particle of flesh had been taken from the bones, even the tough portions of the neck being preserved. The sinews and entrails were saved, the former for making threads for making gloves and clothing, and the latter for casings. The hides were being prepared for tanning; the brains had been eaten; some of the bones had been broken and the marrow taken out and others were being kept to make whip handles and pack-saddle crosstrees. In fact every part of the animal was being utilized either for future food supply or possible source of profit.[344]

The Bannock and Shoshone eventually lost their right to hunt on unoccupied public lands through the trial of Race Horse, a Bannock, who stood trial in proxy for the tribe in a test case to determine whether the 1868 treaty would be upheld. Initially, the courts ruled in favor of the Bannock, but that ruling was appealed to the United States Supreme Court. In a lengthy and complicated argument, the Court concluded that Indians could not hunt on federal lands if they did so in violation of state laws.[345] Once the court found Race Horse guilty, the attorney-general of Wyoming argued convincingly that "this poor Indian should not be further punished." Ironically, they could not find him, as he had joined fellow Bannock and Shoshone on a hunting trip in Jackson's Hole. Eventually, Race Horse was located and returned to face the judge, who instructed him to inform the tribe of the court's findings. Although some Bannock and Shoshone left the reservation to hunt in the Jackson Hole and Yellowstone areas, the Race Horse ruling eventually ended off-reservation hunting in violation of state law.[346] The impact of the loss is apparent in the 1897 report of acting Indian agent F. G. Irwin:

> These Indians have shown no disposition this season to hunt in the Jackson Hole region as has been so long their custom. Their prompt and full compliance with the wishes of the Department in the case is especially commendable, since it results in the loss of a revenue of from $5,000 to $8,000 derived from the proceeds of their annual hunt, and affects nearly every family on the reservation, as they depend entirely upon that source for their supply of buckskin for the manufacture of moccasins, gloves, and various other articles. While the breaking up of this hunting custom must ultimately result in a benefit to the Indians, by forcing them to look to labor as the only means of livelihood, yet it seems just that some recompense should be made to them for the loss of a revenue and privilege clearly secured to them by treaty.[347]

The matter of hunting rights was given some finality in 1897. A Bannock delegation traveled to Washington and "agreed to give up their treaty right to hunt on the public lands of the United States in return for proper compensation . . . [eventually] a provision was included to pay the Indians $75,000 for the relinquishment of their hunting rights."[348]

10

Indians and Yellowstone in the Twentieth Century

The first decades of the twentieth century found native peoples visiting the Yellowstone region for very different reasons than those in the previous hundred years. Dean Green's *History of Island Park* recounts visits to the region just west of Yellowstone in 1912 by Bannock and Shoshone from Fort Hall, including Bannock Chief White Bear.[349] Sam and Ed Eagle note that the same Chief White Bear and his family camped for several consecutive summers in the early 1900s on Hebgen Lake near Rainbow Point,[350] close to traditional camping areas at Corey Springs. These trips are perhaps best characterized as vacations.

During the 1920s, native peoples were invited to participate in official Park events. At the opening of the new West Entrance of the Park on June 18, 1925, for example, a contingent of Shoshone from Fort Hall headed by Chief Tyhee were prominent in the ceremonies. They traveled by train to attend, disembarking at the Union Pacific depot in West Yellowstone. Other political dignitaries included governors Nellie T. Ross (Wyoming), C. C. Moore (Idaho), J. E. Erickson (Montana), and George Dern (Utah).[351] For the Park opening in 1927, Supt. Horace Albright invited White-Man-Runs-Him, the last of Custer's Crow scouts, Max Big Man, an interpreter for the scouts, congressmen Charles C. Winter and John Q. Tilson, and the governor of Wyoming.

Inviting Shoshone and other native peoples to the Park from which they had been systematically banned was consistent with the national trend to associate Indians with parks and wilderness. Superintendent Albright sought to involve Indians in Yellowstone in what might be called performances. In 1925 he invited a group of Crow Indians into the Park to assist in rounding up the Yellowstone bison herd. The Indians wore

Figure 34. Shoshone and Bannock Indians at opening of West Yellowstone Gate Entrance in 1925. (YNP Photo Archives, Neg. No. YELL 37245-1.)

"ancient hunting costumes and rode bareback," attracting tourists who watched the riders chase the bison through the Lamar River Valley. Albright fantasized at the time that the Crow were becoming associated with Yellowstone in the same way that the Blackfeet were a part of Glacier National Park.[352] For several reasons, however, a connection between the Crow and Yellowstone did not develop.

The Blackfeet were the primary aboriginal occupants of the Glacier Park region. In earlier times the Blackfeet had been known as proud hunters and the most feared warriors on the Northern Plains (see Chapter 3 for more on the Blackfeet). Glacier Park became a reality in part through the land cession of 1895 from the Blackfeet Tribe.[353] In addition, Glacier visitation in the early part of the twentieth century was largely via the Great Northern Railroad and that company employed Blackfeet in its hotels. Lavishly-costumed Indians greeted tourists as they left the train, and Winhold Reiss's romantic portraits of Blackfeet leaders and elders adorned Great Northern calendars.[354]

Yellowstone, on the other hand, was not exclusively associated with any one group. Historic use of the region varied among various native peoples—Shoshone, Bannock, Blackfeet, and Crow. If any group was

Figure 35. Indians departing the train at the West Yellowstone Union Pacific depot, 1925. [Clifford Peake photo, author's collection.]

considered the primary occupant of Yellowstone it was the "timid" Sheepeaters, unmounted and feared by few, if any, who offered little to romanticize. The Crow, with their showy costumes and fine horseman-ship, seemed a much better choice and they, like the Blackfeet, had ceded some lands to the Park. Nonetheless, the relationship Albright promoted did not happen. Yellowstone has never been symbolically linked with a specific native group nor with Native Americans generally. Early administrators did their best to advertise the Park as one shunned by Indians over their fear of the geologic features.[355]

After the Nez Perce War of 1877 and the Bannock War of 1878, any real Indian presence in Yellowstone came to an end. The national park status and the importance of tourist visitation demanded that the Park be kept free of any threat of Indian hostilities, or even the possibility of such a threat. As a result, an effective campaign to characterize the park as taboo to the "superstitious" indigenous peoples was launched.

Ironically, the National Park idea as initially conceptualized by George Catlin called for preserving Indians and nature in some roman-tic, frozen moment in the resplendent past:

Figure 36. Horace Albright (fourth from left) with Crow Indians at Gallatin Gateway opening, 1929. (Daum Photo, YNP Photo Archives, Neg. No. YELL 37799-2.)

> What a splendid contemplation too, when one . . . imagines them
> as they *might* in future be seen, (by some great protecting policy
> of government) preserved in their pristine beauty and wildness,
> in a *magnificent park*, where the world could see for ages to come,
> the native Indian in his classic attire, galloping his wild horse,
> with sinewy bow, and shield and lance, amid the fleeting herds of
> elks and buffaloes. What a beautiful and thrilling specimen for
> America to preserve and hold up to the view of her refined citi-
> zens and the world in future ages! *A nation's Park*, containing
> man and beast, in all the wild and freshness of their nature's
> beauty![356] [emphasis, Catlin's]

Catlin sweeps American Indians along with the elk and bison into his
park as "specimens" to be preserved, forever pursuing wild game. This
nineteenth-century attitude, which even foreshadows the racism of the
unilineal evolutionists of the late 1800s,[357] would, of course, be deplored
today. In defense of Catlin, his intentions grew out of a seemingly sin-
cere, albeit nostalgic,[358] desire to protect somehow the pristine West,
including native peoples, from the incessant forces of change that he

Figure 37. Crow chief Max Big Man and his daughter, Myrtle, standing next to Giant Geyser, 1933. (Photo by G. Crowe, YNP Photo Archives, Neg. No. 37806.)

foresaw as destroying his beloved wilderness. Certainly in the case of Yellowstone, Catlin's wishes did not come true. Native peoples were seen at worst as a danger to tourists (who were essential to Park success) and at best as a negative presence that detracted from the enjoyment of the people. Consequently, Park administrators did their best to expel the original inhabitants from its boundaries.[358]

Afterword

The insights into human presence in the Park, obtained through careful archaeological study and diverse historical accounts, enhance our appreciation of Yellowstone's place in the cultural history of North America. Native peoples knew of the many wonders of Yellowstone thousands of years ago. The tendency for whites to believe they were first to be spellbound by the thundering falls, steaming geysers and fumeroles, and scenic beauty of the region is an ethnocentric myth. Archaeological studies in and around Yellowstone demonstrate that the first visitation of the Park began with the dawn of North American human history. Distinctive artifacts and other clues argue that through-out that history Yellowstone and its rich beauty and resources were known and used.

We will never know the thoughts of those earliest visitors as they watched Old Faithful spray its eternal spray, or peered through shifting banks of steam into the richly hued depths of the boiling springs. But we do know that the obsidian from the Park found its way thousands of miles east into the economic and religious life of the ancestors of modern Native Americans and was undoubtedly used by many closer groups for more mundane tool manufacture. We also know that for millennia the Park was a hunting, fishing, and gathering area for native peoples. With each season, bands moved through this game-rich high country in pursuit of sheep, elk, fish, roots, obsidian, and other basics of life. After a day's activities and adventures, they gathered around the evening fire and told and retold accounts of their successes and failures. They knew Yellowstone in a way no modern man ever will.

Notes

[1] William R. Keefer, *The Geologic Story of Yellowstone National Park*, United States Geological Survey Bulletin no. 1347 (Washington : Government Printing Office, 1972).

[2] Robert B. Smith and Lawrence W. Braile, "Topographic Signature, Space-time Evolution, and Physical Properties of the Yellowstone-Snake River Plain Volcanic System : The Yellowstone Hotspot," in ed. A. W. Snoke, J. R. Steidtmann, and S. M. Roberts, *Geology of Wyoming*, Geological Survey of Wyoming Memoir no. 5 (1993), 694–754.

[3] Ibid., 715.

[4] Ibid., 698.

[5] Kenneth L. Pierce, *History and Dynamics of Glaciation in the Northern Yellowstone National Park Area*, Geology of Yellowstone National Park, Geological Survey Professional Paper 729-F (Washington : Government Printing Office, 1979), F30, F65.

[6] Kenneth P. Cannon, George M. Crothers, and Kenneth L. Pierce, *Archaeological Investigations Along the Fishing Bridge Peninsula, Yellowstone National Park, Wyoming : The Archaeology, Geology and Paleoenvironment.* (MSS on file National Park Service, Midwest Archaeological Center, Lincoln, 1994), 9.

[7] Joseph P. Iddings, *Obsidian Cliff, Yellowstone National Park,* United States Geological Survey, Seventh Annual Report (Washington : Government Printing Office, 1972).

[8] Hiram Chittenden, *The Yellowstone National Park*, 5th ed. (Cincinnati : The Robert Clarke Company, 1905), 48–49.

[9] Aubrey L. Haines, *The Yellowstone Story, A History of Our First National Park,* vol. 1 (Mammoth Hot Springs, Wyoming : Yellowstone Library and Museum Association, 1977), 53–59.

[10] John L. Stoddard, *Stoddard's Lectures*, vol. 10, California, Grand Canyon, Yellowstone Park (Chicago : Geo. L. Shuman & Co., 1898), 240–41.

[11] Ibid., 240.

[12] Leslie B. Davis, Stephen A. Aaberg, and James G. Schmitt, *The Obsidian Cliff Plateau Prehistoric Lithic Source, Yellowstone National Park, Wyoming,* Selections

from the Division of Cultural Resources, no. 6. (Denver : National Park Service, Rocky Mountain Region, 1995), 1.

[13] Ibid., various, but especially Chapter 3.

[14] Kenneth P. Cannon and Richard E. Hughes, "Provenance Analysis of Obsidian Paleoindian Projectile Points from Yellowstone National Park, Wyoming," *Current Research in the Pleistocene* 14 (1997) :101–4.

[15] National Park Service, *Yellowstone's Northern Range : Complexity and Change in a Wildland Ecosystem* (Mammoth Hot Springs, Wyoming : Yellowstone National Park, National Park Service, 1997), 22.

[16] Cannon et al., *Fishing Bridge*, 12, and references therein. Also see George C. Frison and Lawrence Todd, *Colby Mammoth Site : Taphonomy and Archaeology of a Clovis Kill in Northern Wyoming* (Albuquerque : University of New Mexico Press, 1986) for evidence of mammoth in the Bighorn Basin of northern Wyoming. See G. Frison, *Prehistoric Hunters of the Plains* (New York : Academic Press, 1991) for additional examples.

[17] Cannon et al., *Fishing Bridge*, 10.

[18] Kenneth P. Cannon, "A Model for Prehistoric Economies of the Yellowstone Plateau During the Altithermal," in *Ecological Implications of Fire in Greater Yellowstone*, ed. J. Greenlee (Fairfield, Washington : International Association of Wildland Fire, 1996), 1–6.

[19] Kenneth L. Pierce, Kenneth P. Cannon, and George M. Crothers, "Archaeological Implications of Changing Levels of Yellowstone Lake, Yellowstone National Park, Wyoming," *Current Research in the Pleistocene* 11 (1994) :106–8. See also Kenneth P. Cannon, Kenneth L. Pierce, and George M. Crothers, "Caldera Unrest, Lake Levels, and Archeology : The View from Yellowstone Lake," *Park Science* 15 (3) :28–32, for more recent discussions on Yellowstone Lake levels.

[20] An exception might be the Little Ice Age that occurred roughly 1350–1870. During this period climates were colder, resulting in glacial advance and shifts in vegetation ranges. See E. C. Peilou, *After the Ice Age : The Return of Life to Glaciated North America* (Chicago : The University of Chicago Press, 1991) for more on this topic.

[21] National Park Service, *Yellowstone's Northern Range,* 46. Charles E. Kay has been a vocal critic of the Park's management of large game and the consequences of that mismanagement on the populations of willow, aspen, beaver, and moose populations. See, for example, Kay, "Is Aspen Doomed ?" *Journal of Forestry* 95 (1997) :4–11, and the various references therein. See also n. 22, below.

[22] The issue of game populations in Yellowstone's past has, indeed, been a topic of lively debate over the past decade. For divergent views see Alton Chase, *Playing God in Yellowstone* (New York : Harcourt Brace Jovanovich, 1987) ; Charles Kay, *Yellowstone's Northern Elk Herd : A Critical Evaluation of the "Natural-Regulation" Paradigm* (Ph.D. diss., Utah State University, 1990) ; Paul Schullery and Lee Whittlesey, "The Documentary Record of Wolves and Related Wildlife

Species in the Yellowstone National Park Area Prior to 1882," in *Wolves for Yellowstone?* ed. J. D. Varley and W. G. Brewster, a report to United States Congress, vol. 4, Research and Analysis, National Park Service, Yellowstone National Park Wyoming (1992), 1–173; National Park Service, *Yellowstone's Northern Range*. Also see the many references in these publications that are primarily concerned with current management of the Park's animal populations, especially elk. The concern in this text is what might have been available for people in the past.

[23] William A. Ferris, *Life in the Rocky Mountains* (Denver: Old West Publishing Co., 1983), 49.

[24] Osborne Russell, *Journal of a Trapper*, ed. Aubrey L. Haines (Portland: Oregon Historical Society, 1955; reprint, Lincoln: University of Nebraska Press, 1965), 44, 66.

[25] Ibid., 63.

[26] The data from Lamar Cave are found in Elizabeth A. Hadly, *Evolution, Ecology, and Taphonomy of Late-Holocene Mammals from Lamar Cave, Yellowstone National Park, Wyoming, USA* (Ph.D. diss., University of California, Berkeley, 1995). The dating of the cave is somewhat problematic (ibid., 13). The earliest levels are dated by radiocarbon to about 3,000 years ago (calibrated) [see n. 37 for more on calibration]. Bison are not present in the upper four levels but were found in modest but consistent numbers from Level 5 down to the bottom of the cave (16 strata). Elk, on the other hand, are more common in the upper levels. See an excellent review of data on bison remains from archaeological sites in and around Yellowstone in Kenneth P. Cannon, *A Review of Prehistoric Faunal Remains from Various Contexts in Yellowstone National Park, Wyoming* (Lincoln: National Park Service, Midwest Archeological Center, 1997). Also see Kenneth P. Cannon, "What the Past Can Provide: Contribution of Prehistoric Bison Studies to Modern Management," *Great Plains Research* 11 (1) (2001).

[27] Russell, 62.

[28] Ferris, 273.

[29] Haines, 81.

[30] Philetus W. Norris, *Annual Report of Superintendent of the Yellowstone National Park to the Secretary of the Interior for the Year 1880* (Washington: Government Printing Office, 1881), 38.

[31] Norris, *Annual Report for 1877*, 843; idem, *1878*, 987.

[32] The history of bison in Yellowstone is nicely detailed in Mary M. Meagher, *The Bison of Yellowstone National Park*, National Park Service, Scientific Monograph Series no. 1 (Washington: Government Printing Office, 1973). More recent treatment of the topic is found in *Yellowstone's Northern Range*, 82–85, and yearly counts are found in Appendix B, of that same volume. See also Cannon, "What the Past Can Provide." These histories tell a complex story of Yellowstone bison populations. Cannon notes that bison numbers in archaeological

sites around the Park fluctuated through time depending on numerous factors. There is no easy answer to "How many bison were there in Yellowstone?"

[33] Russell, various, but see 21.

[34] John C. Fremont, *Memoirs of My Life* (Chicago and New York : Belford, Clark & Company, 1887), 157.

[35] Norris, *1880*, 40. See also William A. Jones, "Report upon Reconnaissance of Northwestern Wyoming made in the Summer of 1873," House Executive Document No. 285, 43rd Congress, 1st Session (Washington : Government Printing Office, 1874) for observations of both elk and mountain sheep in the southeast region of and just outside the Park.

[36] George C. Frison, Charles A. Reher, and Danny N. Walker, "Prehistoric Mountain Sheep Hunting in the Central Rocky Mountains of North America," in ed. Leslie B. Davis and Brian O. K. Reeves, *Hunters of the Recent Past* (London : Unwin Hyman, 1990), 208–40.

[37] Harold McCracken, compiler, *The Mummy Cave Project in Northwestern Wyoming* (Cody, Wyoming : Buffalo Bill Historical Center, 1978), 146–51; Wilfred M. Husted and Robert Edgar, *The Archeology of Mummy Cave Wyoming : An Introduction to Shoshonean Prehistory* (MSS on file, National Park Service, Midwest Archeological Center, Lincoln, n.d.) ; Susan Hughes, personal communication, 1997. An explanation of the abbreviation B.P. is appropriate here. When used in archaeological or other scientific literature, the initials B.P. refer to radiocarbon years before present rather than calendar years. The difference is that radiocarbon years tend to lag behind calendar years, which means that age of an object dated by this technique is actually older than represented by radiocarbon age. The adjustment from radiocarbon years to calendar years is achieved through a comparison to tree-ring dates, which results in a calibrated date. When "years ago" is used here, it means calendar years before the present. B.P. refers to radiocarbon years. The abbreviations B.C. and A.D. refer to calendar years before the birth of Jesus Christ (B.C.) and after his birth (A.D.).

[38] Hadly, 23–25.

[39] Frison et al., "Mountain Sheep Hunting," 228.

[40] Ibid., 223.

[41] Norris, *1880*, 34–36.

[42] See for example, Michael B. Collins, "Forty Years of Archeology in Central Texas," *Bulletin of the Texas Archeological Society* 66 (1995) :388, wherein he correlates wetter climatic conditions and increasing bison remains in Texas archaeological sites.

[43] Hadly, 103.

[44] Cannon, et al., *Fishing Bridge*, 16.

[45] There is no intention here to enter this debate, which tends toward historic management decisions and carrying capacity of Yellowstone. My goal was to explore the resources available to native peoples.

[46] Hadly, 23–25; Yellowstone National Park, *Yellowstone's Northern Range*, 23, 97. See also comments on these and other Park fauna by Norris, *1880*, 38–46.

[47] See Don Despain, *Yellowstone Vegetation: Consequences of Environment and History in a Natural Setting* (Boulder: Roberts Rinehart Publishers, 1990) for excellent coverage of Yellowstone plant life.

[48] Janet L. Dixon, "Indian Uses of Plants," Appendix B in Peter Nabokov and Lawrence Loendorf, *Restoring a Presence: A Documentary Overview of Native Americans and Yellowstone National Park* (Draft report submitted to the National Park Service regional office, Denver, 1999), 434.

[49] See various chapters in Despain.

[50] Gary Wright, *People of the High Country: Jackson Hole Before the Settlers* (New York: Peter Lang, 1984), 5.

[51] See ibid., Table 1 for a partial list of important plants; and Stuart A. Reeve, Thomas E. Marceau, and Gary A. Wright, "Mitigation of the Sheepeater Bridge Site, 48YE320, Yellowstone National Park" (Report submitted to the Midwest Archeological Center, Lincoln, 1980), 4–8, for more discussion of economically important plants in the Park.

[52] See E. James Dixon, *Bones, Boats, & Bison* (Albuquerque: University of New Mexico Press, 1999).

[53] Aubrey L. Haines, *The Yellowstone Story: A History of Our First National Park*, vol. 2 (Mammoth Hot Springs, Wyoming: Yellowstone Library and Museum Association, 1977), 449.

[54] Philetus W. Norris, *Annual Report upon the Yellowstone National Park to the Secretary of the Interior for the Year 1879* (Washington: Government Printing Office, 1880), 9.

[55] Norris, *Fifth Annual Report of the Superintendent of the Yellowstone National Park* (Washington: Government Printing Office, 1881), 34.

[56] Dee C. Taylor, *Preliminary Archaeological Investigations in Yellowstone National Park* (Report generated under contract number 14-10-232-320, a cooperative agreement between the National Park Service and Montana State University, Missoula, 1964), 151–53.

[57] Joel C. Janetski, "The Role of Utah Lake in the Prehistory of Utah Valley," *Utah Historical Quarterly* 58 (1) (1990) :5–31.

[58] Haines, vol. 1, 181.

[59] Davis et al., 247–50.

[60] Ibid.

[61] Haines, vol. 2, 469.

[62] David Condon, "American Indian Burial Giving Evidence of Antiquity Discovered in Yellowstone National Park," *Yellowstone Nature Notes*, (July–August 1948): 37–43. This burial is discussed further under Late Prehistoric Period in Yellowstone later in this chapter.

[63] Wayne F. Replogle, *Yellowstone's Bannock Indian Trails* (Mammoth Hot Springs, Wyoming: Yellowstone Library and Museum Association, 1956).

[64] Two reports came from this research. J. Jacob Hoffman, *A Preliminary Archeological Survey of Yellowstone National Park* (MA thesis, Montana State University, 1961); Taylor, cited in n.56.

[65] Hoffman, 40.

[66] The two primary reports on Mummy Cave are McCracken, and Husted and Edgar, cited in n.37. Susan Hughes's recent research focuses on the animal bones. The brief historical comments presented here are from those volumes. See Susan Hughes, "Mummy Cave Revisited," *Annals of Wyoming* 60 (2) (1988):44–54; and Susan Hughes, "Synthesis of the Mummy Cave Materials: 1994" (MSS on file, Bureau of Land Management, Worland, Wyoming, 1994).

[67] See references to Susan Hughes's work in n.66.

[68] Gary A. Wright, "Archeological Research in Yellowstone National Park," *Thirty-Third Annual Field Conference, Wyoming Geological Association Guidebook* (1982), 11.

[69] The works here are several, but most important is Gary Wright, *People of the High Country*; Reeve et al.; Gary Wright, Susan Bender, and Stuart Reeve, "High Country Adaptations," *Plains Anthropologist* 25 (89) (1988):181–97. See also Anne E. Samuelson, *Archaeological Investigations in the Grant Village–West Thumb Area of Yellowstone National Park, Wyoming* (Masters Thesis, State University of New York at Albany, 1981). For more on the contributions of these individuals see references in these publications.

[70] For the best overview and excellent references on this research see Davis, et al. [n.12].

[71] Mack W. Shortt, "Museum of the Rockies Archaeological Research in the Canyons of the Yellowstone," *Yellowstone Science* 9 (2) (Spring 2001):16–20.

[72] Cannon, et al., *Fishing Bridge*.

[73] Cannon's publications are many but two are characteristic. Cannon, *A Review of Prehistoric Faunal Remains*; Kenneth P. Cannon and Richard E. Hughes, "The Continuing Obsidian Studies in the Greater Yellowstone Area" (Paper presented at the 62nd Annual Meeting of the Society for American Archeology, Nashville, 1997).

[74] Shortt, 16–20.

[75] See E. James Dixon for more on Paleoindian sites in North America.

[76] See various chapters in ed. Warren L. d'Azevedo, gen. ed. William C. Sturtevant, *Great Basin*, Handbook of North American Indians, vol. 11 (Washington: Smithsonian Institution, 1986), for more on the archaeology of the Great Basin.

[77] J. J. Hester, *Blackwater Locality No. 1: A Stratified Early Man Site in Eastern New Mexico*, Publication no. 8 (Ranchos de Taos, New Mexico: Fort Burgwin Research Center, 1972).

[78] For more on Clovis technology, see A. T. Boldurain, and J. L. Cotter, *Clovis Revisited: New Perspectives on Paleoindian Adaptations from Blackwater Draw, New Mexico* (Philadelphia: University Museum, University of Pennsylvania, 1999); Michael B. Collins, *Clovis Blade Technology* (Austin: University of Texas Press,

1999). The term "projectile point" is a generalized label used by archaeologists to refer to the chipped stone tools used to tip atlatl darts, spears, and arrows when the exact function of the tool is not known. In contrast, "arrowhead" refers to projectile points used to tip arrows. Arrowheads are significantly smaller than points and appeared in western North America about 2,000 years ago.

[79] Frison.

[80] Haines, vol. 1, 16. Apparently the whereabouts of this important artifact is now unknown and not available for sourcing analysis, although photographs are available. See Davis et al., 49, for more details.

[81] Larry Lahren, "Bone Foreshafts from a Clovis Burial in Southwestern Montana," *Science* (October 1974) :147–50. Portions of the collection from this site are on exhibit at the Montana Historical Society in Helena.

[82] Frison and Todd.

[83] Cannon et al., *Fishing Bridge*, 40.

[84] Leslie B. Davis and Sally T. Greiser, "Indian Creek Paleoindians : Early Occupation of the Elkhorn Mountains' Southeast Flank, West-Central Montana," in ed. Dennis Stanford and Jane S. Day, *Ice Hunters of the Rockies* (Denver : Denver Museum of Natural History and University Press of Colorado, 1992), 225–83. Although no obsidian points were found at Indian Creek, obsidian flakes from Late Paleoindian levels were sourced to both Obsidian Cliffs and Bear Gulch in southern Idaho.

[85] B. Robert Butler, "Prehistory of the Snake and Salmon River Area," in ed. Warren L. d'Azevedo, gen. ed. William C. Sturtevant, *Great Basin*, Handbook of North American Indians, vol. 11 (Washington : Smithsonian Institution, 1986), 127–34, contains a nice summary of the early archaeology of the Snake River region.

[86] See Dee C. Taylor and George C. Frison for more on the Cody Complex.

[87] McCracken.

[88] Cannon et al., *Fishing Bridge*, 132.

[89] M. A. Conner, "Site Testing at Jackson Lake : A Jackson Lake Archaeological Interim Report" (MSS on file Midwest Archeological Center, Lincoln, 1987).

[90] Davis et al., 51.

[91] Cannon and Hughes, "Provenance Analysis," 101–4. The points were sourced to Bear Gulch, Pack Saddle Creek in eastern Idaho, and Obsidian Cliff.

[92] Cannon et al., *Fishing Bridge*, 43.

[93] Aubrey L. Haines, "Preliminary Report on the Rigler Bluffs Prehistoric Indian Site, 24PA401" (MSS on file, Yellowstone National Park Archives, Mammoth, 1962).

[94] Reeve et al. Archaeologists resorted to the use of obsidian hydration in the absence of charcoal for the more standard radiocarbon dating on this project. Briefly, obsidian hydration dates are derived from measuring the thickness of a rind that forms on freshly exposed obsidian due to the absorption of water. There are a number of complicating variables in this dating technique.

⁹⁵ Stuart A. Reeve, Gary A. Wright, Thomas E. Marceau, and Priscilla Mecham, "Archaeological Investigations of the Lawrence Site (48TE509) Grand Teton National Park, Wyoming" (MSS on file, Department of Anthropology, State University of New York, Albany, 1979). The earliest radiocarbon date from the Lawrence Site is about 2000 B.P. The authors strongly suspect the importance of root crops has much greater time depth.

⁹⁶ See also Gary A. Wright, *People of the High Country*.

⁹⁷ Reeve et al., "Lawrence Site," 30. The authors describe in detail the process of roasting root plants such as camas that required the use of rocks to hold the heat. After the rocks were heated they tended to break up, requiring the processors to rake the fragmented stones out of the oven and replace them with a fresh supply. This process resulted in piles of fire-cracked rock encircling the ovens.

⁹⁸ Reeve et al., "Lawrence Site," 58.

⁹⁹ Gordon R. Willey and Jeremy A. Sabloff, *History of American Archaeology*, 2nd ed. (New York: W. H. Freeman and Company, 1993).

¹⁰⁰ Davis et al., 56. Holmes's reference to rouletted ware or surface decorated pottery is intriguing and could suggest the presence of ceramics from the eastern woodlands. Little is known of the specimen Holmes references. Some surface decorated pottery is known from the region. Cannon et al., *Fishing Bridge*, 52.

¹⁰¹ James B. Griffen, A. A. Gordus, and G. A. Wright, "Identification of Hopewellian Obsidian in the Middle West," *American Antiquity* 34 (1) (1969):1–14. For additional information on the blades in Figure 8, see W. K. Moorehead, "The Hopewell Mound Group of Ohio," Chicago Field Museum of Natural History Publication 211, Anthropological Series 6 (5).

¹⁰² The reference for Yellowstone obsidian in Iowa is Duane C. Anderson, Joseph A. Tiffany, and Fred W. Nelson, "Recent Research on Obsidian from Iowa Archaeological Sites," *American Antiquity* 41 (1986):837–52; for North Dakota, Fred W. Nelson, personal communication (1986); for Oklahoma, Griffen et al.

¹⁰³ Davis et al., 53–55.

¹⁰⁴ Joel C. Janetski, "Transitions in Eastern Great Basin Prehistory," in ed. David B. Madsen and David Rhode, *Across the West: Human Population Movement and the Expansion of the Numa* (Salt Lake City: University of Utah Press, 1994), 157–78.

¹⁰⁵ Davis et al, 51–52.

¹⁰⁶ George C. Frison, *The Wardell Buffalo Trap 48SU301: Communal Procurement in the Upper Green River Basin, Wyoming*, Anthropological Papers no. 48 (Ann Arbor: Museum of Anthropology, University of Michigan, 1973), 74.

¹⁰⁷ Taylor, 70–73.

¹⁰⁸ Norris, *Fifth Annual Report*, 33–34.

¹⁰⁹ See section on Previous Archaeological Research above and discussion of the discovery of steatite vessels around Yellowstone in Taylor, 147–49.

¹¹⁰ Thomas E. Marceau, "Steatite, Intermountain Pottery and the Shoshone: Problems in Association" (Paper presented at the 39th Annual Plains Confer-

ence, Bismarck, North Dakota, 1981). Marceau concludes that the makers of Intermountain pottery and steatite vessels were not the same ethnic group.

[111] Shortt, 18–19.

[112] Condon, 37–43.

[113] For more on the arrival of the bow and arrow on the Plains see Frison, *Prehistoric Hunters*. For a discussion of arrow points in the Great Basin and on the Snake River Plain, see Richard N. Holmer, "Common Projectile Points of the Intermountain West," in ed. Carol J. Condie and Don D. Fowler, *Anthropology of the Desert West* (Salt Lake City: University of Utah Press, 1986), 89–115; Richard N. Holmer, "In Search of the Ancestral Shoshone," in ed. David B. Madsen and David Rhode, *Across the West: Human Population Movement and the Expansion of the Numa* (Salt Lake City, University of Utah Press, 1994), 179–87.

[114] Taylor, 114, 121; Cannon et al., *Fishing Bridge*, 50. Wright, "Archeological Research in Yellowstone National Park,"12, reported obsidian hydration dates on unidentified artifacts that suggest the burial pit was constructed about 3,000 years ago. The presence of arrow points argues against these dates being reliable. Wright also contradicts Condon's sexing of the burial, a conclusion that Cannon et al., *Fishing Bridge*, 32, refute based on more recent work that suggests Wright confused the 1941 burial with the 1956 remains reported here in the following paragraph. For more on this issue see Gary A. Wright, R. Proulx, and T. Koenig, "A Native American Burial from 48YE1, Fishing Bridge Peninsula, Yellowstone National Park," *Wyoming Archaeologist* (1982).

[115] Cannon et al., *Fishing Bridge*, 32.

[116] Ibid.,. 50–51.

[117] It is important to credit the work of Ake Hultkrantz, "The Indians of Yellowstone Park," *Annals of Wyoming* 29 (2) (1957):125–49. The format here follows generally that of his early article.

[118] Francis Haines, "Northward Spread of Horses to the Plains Indians," *American Anthropologist* 40 (3) (1938):429–37.

[119] Ibid. See also Mark Sutton, "Warfare and Expansion," *Journal of California and Great Basin Anthropology* 8 (1) (1986):65–82.

[120] Uto-Aztekan speakers in the Great Basin and immediately adjacent areas have been divided into Western, Central, and Southern Numic language groups by anthropologists. The term "Numic" is derived from the word *neme, newe,* or *numa* which is the term Shoshone or Southern Paiutes used to refer to themselves, and means "the people." See Wick Miller, "Anthropological Linguistics in the Great Basin," in ed. W. L. d'Azevedo et al., *The Current Status of Anthropological Research in the Great Basin: 1964*, Desert Research Institute Social Sciences and Humanities Publications 1 (Reno: University of Nevada, 1966), 75–112. Western Numic refers primarily to the language of the Northern Paiute and related groups of the western Great Basin. Central Numic is the language of the Western, Northern, and Eastern Shoshone of Nevada, Utah, Idaho, and western Wyoming. Southern Numic is spoken primarily by the Ute and

Southern Paiute of Utah, Colorado, and parts of Arizona and Nevada. These languages are closely related, but are not mutually intelligible. A Ute speaking Southern Numic, for example, has about as much difficulty communicating with a Central Numic speaking Northern Shoshone as a Frenchman has speaking with an Italian. For an excellent discussion, see Wick R. Miller, "Numic Languages," in ed. Warren L. d'Azevedo, gen. ed. William C. Sturtevant, *Great Basin*, Handbook of North American Indians, vol. 11 (Washington : Smithsonian Institution, 1986), 98–106.

[121] F. Haines, 429–37.

[122] John C. Ewers, *The Blackfeet* (Norman : University of Oklahoma Press, 1971), 5.

[123] Ibid., 125.

[124] Ibid.,126–27.

[125] Russell, 101–2.

[126] Ewers, 66.

[127] Russell, 89.

[128] Doane later served in Yellowstone Park and commanded the military escort for the Washburn-Doane Expedition through the Yellowstone region. In 1889 he applied to be superintendent of the Park. His personal account of this event is found in Orrin H. Bonney and Lorraine Bonney, *Battle Drums and Geysers* (Chicago : Swallow Press, 1970), 22–25.

[129] Robert H. Keller and Michael F. Turek, *American Indians and National Parks* (Tucson : University of Arizona Press, 1998), 51.

[130] Horace Albright, *Oh, Ranger! A Book about the National Parks* (Stanford : Stanford University Press, 1928), 89. He calls the Blackfeet the "Indians of Glacier Park," reflecting their perceived and real historic connection with that part of the country.

[131] Keller and Turek, 62.

[132] John C. Ewers, *The Horse in Blackfoot Indian Culture,* Bureau of American Ethnology Bulletin 159 (Washington : Smithsonian Institution, 1955), 8.

[133] Siouan is the term used by linguists to refer to a group of related Indian languages spoken by such groups as the Dakota or Sioux tribes (e.g., Teton, Yankton, Sisseton), Mandan, Assiniboine, Osage, Omaha, Crow, and Hidatsa.

[134] Edwin Thompson Denig, *Five Indian Tribes of the Upper Missouri* (Norman : University of Oklahoma Press, 1961), 65.

[135] Russell, 146.

[136] Bonney and Bonney, 65.

[137] For more on this issue see Richard A. Bartlett, *Yellowstone, A Wilderness Besieged* (Tucson : University of Arizona Press, 1985), 226; Keller and Turek, 22–23.

[138] Gary A. Wright, "The Shoshonean Migration Problem," *Plains Anthropologist* 23 (1978) :113–37. See Holmer, "Ancestral Shoshone," for a contrary view and Miller, "Numic Languages," for the linguistic perspective.

[139] Sidney M. Lamb, "Linguistic Prehistory in the Great Basin," *International Journal of American Linguistics* 24 (2) (1958) :95–100; David B. Madsen, "Dating Paiute-Shoshone Expansion in the Great Basin," *American Antiquity* 40 (1) (1975) :82–86. For more complete recent histories of the Shoshone and Bannock see Brigham D. Madsen, *The Lemhi : Sacajawea's People* (Caldwell, Idaho : Caxton Press, 1979); Brigham D. Madsen, *The Northern Shoshoni* (Caldwell, Idaho : The Caxton Printers, Ltd., 1980); Robert F. Murphy and Yolanda Murphy, *Shoshone-Bannock Subsistence and Society*, University of California Anthropological Papers 16 (7) (1960) :292–338. For a recent, mostly archaeological discussion of the pros and cons of the Numic Spread across the Great Basin, see the various chapters in David B. Madsen and David Rhode, *Across the West* (Salt Lake City : University of Utah Press, 1994).

[140] The name Lemhi is derived from Mormon settlers who established a mission on the Salmon River in 1855. They named the mission after King Limhi, a character in the *Book of Mormon*. The settlers began referring to the native Shoshone in the area as the Lemhi Indians and the name stuck. See B. Madsen, *The Lemhi*, 35–36.

[141] For some discussions of the origins of the term Snake used to refer to the Indians of southern Idaho, see Brigham D. Madsen, *The Bannock of Idaho* (Caldwell, Idaho : Caxton Press, 1958), 19; Virginia Cole Trenholm and Maurice Carley, *The Shoshonis, Sentinels of the Rockies* (Norman : University of Oklahoma Press, 1964), 3–4.

[142] See various discussions of the use of this term in Julian H. Steward, *Basin Plateau Aboriginal Sociopolitical Groups*, Bureau of American Ethnology Bulletin no. 120 (Washington : Government Printing Office, 1938; reprint, Salt Lake City : University of Utah Press, 1997).

[143] Steward, 186.

[144] For excellent insights into the origin and implications of these food-named groups, see Catherine Fowler, "Food Named Groups among Northern Paiute in North America's Great Basin : An Ecological Interpretation," in ed. N. Williams and E. Hunn, *Resource Managers : North American and Australian Hunter-gatherers* (Boulder : American Association for the Advancement of Science Selected Symposium 67, 1982), 113–29

[145] B. Madsen, *The Lemhi*, 23.

[146] Steward, 198.

[147] See B. Madsen, *The Bannock of Idaho*, 18; Steward, 1938, 198; Sven Liljeblad, "Indian Peoples in Idaho" (MSS on file, Idaho State University, 1957), 82, for additional discussion of the origin and meaning of the term Bannock. Liljeblad published a shorter version (with the same name) of this manuscript in ed. Merill D. Beal and Merle W. Wells, *History of Idaho* (New York : Lewis Historical Publishing Company, Inc. 1959), 29–59. The references in this text to Liljeblad's work on Idaho's native people is to the longer, original manuscript.

[148] Liljeblad, 61.

[149] Karen Lupo, "The Historical Occurrence and Demise of Bison in Northeastern Utah," *Utah Historical Quarterly* 64 (2) (1996) :168–180.

[150] Steward, 186. Wick Miller's useful publication *Newe Natekwinappeh : Shoshoni Stories and Dictionary*, Anthropological Papers no. 94 (Salt Lake City : University of Utah Press, 1972) lists "tukku" as meaning "meat, flesh, or mountain sheep." Interestingly, none of the other large game animals—deer, elk, antelope—are called "tukku" or meat. This could suggest that mountain sheep were an important source of meat for all Shoshone.

[151] Ake Hultkrantz, "The Shoshones in the Rocky Mountain Area," *Annals of Wyoming* 33 (1) (1961) :34.

[152] Aubrey L. Haines, *Yellowstone National Park, Its Exploration and Establishment* (Washington : National Park Service, U.S. Department of the Interior, 1974), 48.

[153] Wright, "The Shoshonean Migration Problem," 113. See notes in Chapter 3 regarding the debate surrounding the timing of the arrival of Shoshone speakers.

[154] Susan Hughes has written a fascinating paper that details how these early impressions were combined with the biases of the nineteenth century to construct a portrait of the Sheepeaters that was based less on reality than on bias. To read more see Susan Hughes, "The Sheepeater Myth of Northwestern Wyoming," *Plains Anthropologist* 45 (171) (2000) :63–83.

[155] Washington Irving, "Astoria," in *The Works of Washington Irving*, vol. 2 (New York : Peter Fenelon Collier, Publisher, n.d.), 370.

[156] David Dominick, "The Sheepeaters," *Annals of Wyoming* 36 (2) (1964) : 132–68.

[157] Russell, 26.

[158] Norris, *1880*, 35.

[159] Taylor, 33.

[160] Liljeblad, 95–96.

[161] Ibid., 99.

[162] Wright, *People of the High Country*, 92.

[163] Wright et al., "High Country Adaptations," 190–91.

[164] Wright, *People of the High Country*, 93.

[165] Dominick, 140.

[166] Harrison Fuller, "Report for Lemhi Special Indian Agency," in *Annual Report of the Commissioner of Indian Affairs to the Secretary of the Interior for the Year 1876* (Washington : Government Printing Office, 1876), 44; John A. Wright, "Report for Lemhi Special Indian Agency, Idaho," in *Annual Report of the Commissioner of Indian Affairs to the Secretary of the Interior for the Year 1878* (Washington : Government Printing Office, 1878), 51.

[167] See Liljeblad; Julian H. Steward, "Culture Element Distributions : XXIII Northern and Gosiute Shoshone," *Anthropological Records* 8 (3) (1945) : 263–392.

[168] See, for example, Steward, "Northern and Gosiute Shoshone," 278–79.

169 Liljeblad, 35.

170 Ake Hultkrantz, "Mythology and Religious Concepts," in ed. Warren L. d'Azevedo, gen. ed. William C. Sturtevant, *Great Basin*, Handbook of North American Indians, vol. 11 (Washington : Smithsonian Institution, 1986), 636.

171 Steward, "Northern and Gosiute Shoshone," 280–81, 342.

172 Liljeblad, "Indian Peoples in Idaho," 35 and Steward, "Northern and Gosiute Shoshone," 278.

173 Steward, "Northern and Gosiute Shoshone," 377.

174 Hultkrantz, "Mythology and Religious Concepts," 637.

175 Ake Hultkrantz, a Swedish ethnographer, is widely recognized as the foremost authority on the Sheepeaters and especially Sheepeater religious beliefs. This paper treats this topic briefly. For more detail see Hultkrantz, "Mythology and Religious Concepts," and the many references within that volume.

176 Steward, "Gosiute and Northern Shoshone," 286.

177 Ibid.

178 Demitri B. Shimkin, "Eastern Shoshoni," in ed. Warren L. d'Azevedo, gen. ed. William C. Sturtevant, *Great Basin*, Handbook of North American Indians, vol. 11 (Washington : Smithsonian Institution, 1986), 325.

179 Sven Liljeblad, "Oral Tradition : Content and Style of Verbal Arts," in ed. Warren L. d'Azevedo, gen. ed. William C. Sturtevant, *Great Basin*, Handbook of North American Indians, vol. 11 (Washington : Smithsonian Institution, 1986), 653–54.

180 Hultkrantz, "Mythology and Religious Concepts," 636.

181 David H. Thomas, Lori S. A. Pendelton, and S. C. Cappannari, "Western Shoshone," in ed. Warren L. d'Azevedo, gen. ed. William C. Sturtevant, *Great Basin*, Handbook of North American Indians, vol. 11 (Washington : Smithsonian Institution, 1986), 269.

182 Frison, et al., 208–40.

183 Ibid., 233–34.

184 Shimkin, 325.

185 See, for example, George Frison, *Prehistoric Hunters of the High Plains* (New York : Academic Press, 1978), 75.

186 Liljeblad, "Indian Peoples in Idaho," 97.

187 Ibid., 98.

188 Russell, 27. See S. Hughes, "Sheepeater Myth," 75 for a reference from Henderson's 1866 journal, wherein he recounts an encounter with "Sheepeaters" and traded with them for sheep and marten furs.

189 Dominick, 155.

190 See T. M. Hamilton, *Native American Bows* (York, Pennsylvania : George Shumway Publisher, 1972) for excellent discussions of sheep horn and other horn bows among people of the Plains and Intermountain region. Elkhorn was also used to make bows that were likewise very powerful. Hamilton quotes Alfred Jacob Miller on p. 97, "with an Elk-horn bow, they (name of tribe not given,

but most likely a Plains tribe in the Upper Missouri region) sometimes drive an arrow completely through a Buffalo." He also quotes a Hidatsa named Wolf-chief who maintained that a bow made from ram's horn was superior to one made from elk horn, 94–96.

[191] Liljeblad, "Indian Peoples in Idaho," 96.

[192] Vessel blanks are large chunks of steatite that have been roughly shaped but not completely finished into the final vessel form. See Frison, *Prehistoric Hunters* (1991) for a discussion of steatite vessel finds in Wyoming.

[193] Dominick, 162.

[194] Norris, *1880*, 35–36.

[195] Frison, *Prehistoric Hunters* (1991), 264. Also Frison et al., "Prehistoric Mountain Sheep Hunting," various.

[196] Liljeblad, "Indian Peoples in Idaho," 97.

[197] Murphy and Murphy, 310.

[198] Various, but see Dawn S. Statham, *Camas and the Northern Shoshoni : A Biogeographic and Socioeconomic Analysis*, Archaeological Reports no. 10 (Boise : Boise State University, 1982) ; G. Wright, *People of the High Country*, 10.

[199] Liljeblad, "Indian Peoples in Idaho," 96.

[200] Norris, *1880*, 3.

[201] Norris, *1881*, 45. Hultkrantz, "Indians in Yellowstone," 145 recounts this action by Norris and continues, "The treaties were ratified by the Congress in 1882." However, Keller and Turek, 249, n.8, report that no such treaty documents are known.

[202] Haines, vol. 1, 201. See Hughes, "Sheepeater Myth," 76, for a discussion of Togwatee's lack of knowledge of the interior of the Park.

[203] Bartlett, 30–33.

[204] Ake Hultkrantz, *The Indians in Yellowstone National Park* (New York : Garland Press, 1974), 235. See also Haines, vol. 1, 279–80 for a description of the Chester Arthur party, although the role of the Sheepeaters is not mentioned.

[205] Ray H. Grassley, *Pacific Northwest Indian Wars* (Portland : Binfords & Mort Publishers, 1953), 239–40. See also John Wright, "Lemhi Indian Agent Report," *Annual Report to the Commissioner of Indian Affairs* (1879), 54, for concerns about the negative influence of the Bannock.

[206] Grassley, 243.

[207] B. Madsen, *The Lemhi*, 103.

[208] Grassley, 247.

[209] Ibid., 246.

[210] Ibid., 247, reports that 65 Sheepeaters were captured between September 21 and October 9. B. Madsen, *The Lemhi*, 104, on the other hand, cites Howard's report, which states that Farrow captured 51 Indians, including 15 warriors. Grassley does not break these numbers down by sex or age.

[211] B. Madsen, *Lemhi Shoshoni*, 104.

[212] Ibid., 24.

²¹³ This history has been recounted numerous times and this brief version depends heavily on Mark H. Brown, *The Flight of the Nez Perce* (New York : G. P. Putnam Sons, 1967) ; and Alvin Josephy, *The Nez Perce and the Opening of the Northwest* (New Haven : Yale University Press, 1965). Other references are cited as appropriate in the narration.

²¹⁴ Just above the mouth of Lolo Creek the Nez Perce encountered a crude log barricade hastily constructed across the canyon by a group of enlisted men and civilian volunteers under the direction of Capt. Charles C. Rawn of the Seventh Cavalry stationed at Fort Missoula. Backed by his small group of regulars and volunteers, Rawn attempted to detain the Indians, but they simply detoured over the mountain and avoided the obstacle. His feeble barricade was jokingly nicknamed "Fort Fizzle" by amused locals.

²¹⁵ This is Looking Glass Jr. (Allalimya Takanin) whose father (Meiway Apash Wyakaikt) had been an important leader of the Nez Perce, and died during the winter of 1862–63. Looking Glass Jr. was not as powerful a leader as his father and during the course of the Nez Perce War lost and resumed leadership of the band. For more detail on Looking Glass Jr. see Josephy, especially 403. Additional information on Looking Glass, both Sr. and Jr., can be found in Francis Haines, *The Nez Perces* (Norman : University of Oklahoma Press, 1955).

²¹⁶ See William L. Lang's "Where Did the Nez Perces Go in Yellowstone in 1877 ?" *Montana, The Magazine of Western History* (Winter 1990) :18–19 especially for a discussion of this issue of whether or not the Nez Perce were unfamiliar with Yellowstone. For example, see White Hawk's comments in Chapter 5.

²¹⁷ Mark H. Brown, "Yellowstone Tourists and the Nez Perce," *Montana Magazine of Western History* 16 (3) (1966) :34.

²¹⁸ Ibid., 36.

²¹⁹ Lang, 28, reports that Irwin escaped.

²²⁰ Paul Schullery, "Mrs. George Cowan 1877," in *Old Yellowstone Days* (Boulder : Associated University Press, 1979), 11–12.

²²¹ Lang, 19. The discussion of the Nez Perce route is also taken from Lang.

²²² Ibid., 21.

²²³ Ibid., see especially the map, 21, and discussion on 28–29.

²²⁴ Ibid., 22–23.

²²⁵ Ibid., 20.

²²⁶ Josephy, 594.

²²⁷ Ibid., 608.

²²⁸ Ibid., 609.

²²⁹ Ibid., 612.

²³⁰ Ibid., 623.

²³¹ See Josephy, especially the Epilogue, for excellent coverage of the postwar period and Joseph's efforts. The speech made by Joseph to Congress in 1879 is every bit as stirring as "Fight No More Forever," and is worth reading.

²³² Statham, 73.

[233] Steward, *Basin-Plateau Sociopolitical Groups*, 6, and various other references in the text.

[234] J. B. Monteith, "Reports of Agents in Idaho, Office Indian Agent Nez Perce Indians," in *Annual Report of the Commissioner of Indian Affairs to the Department of the Interior for the Year 1876* (Washington: Government Printing Office, 1876), 45; W. V. Rinehart, "Reports of Agents in Oregon, Malheur Indian Agency, Oregon," in *Annual Report of the Commissioner of Indian Affairs to the Department of the Interior for the Year 1876* (Washington: Government Printing Office, 1876), 121.

[235] Steward, *Basin-Plateau Sociopolitical Groups*, 45.

[236] Brigham D. Madsen, *The Northern Shoshoni* (Caldwell, Idaho: The Caxton Printers, Ltd., 1980), 49.

[237] Ibid., 52.

[238] The substitution of "Kansas" for "Camas" is thought to be a clerical mistake, but it had serious consequences for the Bannock.

[239] B. Madsen, *Northern Shoshoni*, 80.

[240] George F. Brimlow, *The Bannock Indian War of 1878* (Caldwell, Idaho: Caxton Printers, Ltd., 1938).

[241] W. H. Danilson, "Report of Agents in Idaho, Fort Hall Indian Agency," *Annual Report of the Commissioner of Indian Affairs to the Secretary of the Interior for the Year 1876* (Washington: Government Printing Office, 1876), 43.

[242] W. V. Rinehart, "Reports of Agents in Oregon, Malheur Agency, Oregon," *Annual Report of the Commissioner of Indian Affairs to the Secretary of the Interior for the Year 1877* (Washington: Government Printing Office, 1877), 174.

[243] John A. Wright, *1878*, 51.

[244] John A. Wright, "Reports of Agents in Idaho, Lemhi Indian Agency, Idaho," *Annual Report of the Commissioner of Indian Affairs to the Secretary of the Interior for the Year 1879* (Washington: Government Printing Office, 1879), 55.

[245] Brimlow, 61.

[246] Rinehart, *1877*, 79.

[247] Liljeblad, "Indian Peoples in Idaho," 74.

[248] Brimlow, 67.

[249] Ibid., 73–74.

[250] B. Madsen, *The Bannock*, 206.

[251] Brimlow, 70.

[252] Ibid., 80.

[253] Liljeblad, "Indian Peoples in Idaho" (1957), 76.

[254] Brimlow, 108.

[255] B. Madsen, *The Bannock*, 218, refers to Oytes as a Paiute prophet and dreamer who wanted war. Nabokov and Loendorf, *Restoring a Presence*, 270, note that Oytes assumed leadership of the hostile Indians after the death of Egan but surrendered on August 12.

[256] B. Madsen, *The Bannock*, 218. Apparently the death of Buffalo Horn was a significant catalyst in inflaming the hostiles to action. See Brimlow, 92.

[257] B. Madsen, *The Bannock*, 221.

[258] Bartlett, 27.

[259] Brimlow, 180.

[260] Bartlett, 28.

[261] Norris, *1878*, 980. Beaver Lake, which once lay at the foot of Obsidian Cliff, is now largely grassed over and hardly a lake at all. The photo of the cliff and lake in Chapter 1 shows these natural features much as they would have been in Norris's time.

[262] Haines, vol. 1, 238.

[263] Brimlow, 183.

[264] B. Madsen, *The Bannock*, 225.

[265] Bartlett, 28.

[266] Statham, 24.

[267] Liljeblad, "Indian Peoples in Idaho," 78.

[268] Russell, 123.

[269] Ferris, 323.

[270] Ibid., 326.

[271] Russell, 36.

[272] Lupo, 168–80.

[273] Russell, 39.

[274] Ibid., 36.

[275] Steward, *Basin-Plateau Sociopolitical Groups*, 200.

[276] Chittenden, 9. See also Merrill D. Beal, *The Story of Man in Yellowstone National Park* (Yellowstone National Park : Yellowstone Library and Museum Association, 1960), 87; William A. Jones, *Report upon Reconnaissance of Northwestern Wyoming made in the Summer of 1873*, House Executive Document No. 285, 43rd Congress, 1st Session (Washington : Government Printing Office, 1874), 54–55, for comments on trails south of Yellowstone.

[277] Chittenden, 9.

[278] Beal, *Man in Yellowstone*, 88.

[279] Liljeblad, "Indian Peoples in Idaho," 63–65.

[280] For more information on the Bannock Trail see Replogle; Aubrey L. Haines, *The Bannock Indian Trail* (Yellowstone National Park : Yellowstone Library and Museum Association, 1964) ; and Nabokov and Loendorf, Appendix A.

[281] Norris, *1877*, 842.

[282] George W. Wingate, *Through the Yellowstone Park on Horseback* (New York : O. Judd Co., 1886), 139.

[283] Reau Campbell, *Campbell's New Revised Complete Guide and Descriptive Book of the Yellowstone Park* (Chicago : Rogers and Smith Co., 1913), 37.

[284] Ibid.

[285] Beal, *Man in Yellowstone*, 328.

[286] Joseph Weixelman, *The Power to Evoke Wonder : Native Americans & the Geysers of Yellowstone National Park* (Masters thesis, Montana State University, 1992), 60.

[287] Ferris, 328.

[288] Ake Hultkrantz, "The Fear of Geysers among Indians of the Yellowstone Park Area," in ed. Leslie B. Davis, *Lifeways of Intermontane and Plains Indians*, Museum of the Rockies, Occasional Papers no. 1 (1979), 35.

[289] Haines, vol. 1, 89–90.

[290] Bonney and Bonney, 334.

[291] Norris, *Fifth Annual Report*, 38.

[292] Both the Sheridan and Burnett accounts are in Hultkrantz, "Fear of Geysers," 36.

[293] Haines, vol. 1, 218.

[294] Ake Hultkrantz, "The Indians and the Wonders of Yellowstone : A Study of the Interrelations of Religion, Nature and Culture" *Ethnos* 1 (1954). Hultkrantz concluded that the fear of the geysers was in fact a kind of taboo based on a fear of malevolent spirits believed to dwell there. In "Fear of Geysers," he relaxes this position somewhat. But see discussion later in this chapter regarding water babies.

[295] Hultkrantz, "Fear Of Geysers," 37. See also Weixelman, 57.

[296] Hultkrantz, "Fear of Geysers," 37.

[297] Weixelman, 36.

[298] Norris, *1880*, 35.

[299] Norris, *Fifth Annual Report*, 32–38.

[300] Taylor, 46-49. Of course, this comment was made three decades ago and much more of the Park's archaeological resources are known. For more recent overviews, see Cannon et al., *Fishing Bridge*; Shortt; Chapter 2 of this volume.

[301] Nabokov and Loendorf, Appendix A. Hultkrantz, "Indians of Yellowstone," 57–60, argues that trails avoided the geysers. See Hultkrantz, "Fear of Geysers," 38, for a partial recanting of this position based on archaeological work subsequent to his 1954 article. Weixelman, 29, also contains a map of the Native American trails in Yellowstone.

[302] Noted ethnographer of the Blackfeet, John C. Ewers, relates how a young man in search of power isolated himself, usually on "a bare hilltop, beside a lake, or in some other rarely frequented place" and fasted and prayed to the "powers of sky, earth, and water." Supplications invoked those powers as follows: "Hear, Sun; hear, Old Man; Above People, listen; Underwater People, listen" [Ewers, *The Blackfeet*, 162–63]. The importance of water and spirits or power that dwelt in water is apparent in this appeal. Julian Steward also discusses the pursuit of shamanistic dreams or visions through fasting, especially in the mountains, and speculates that this kind of behavior may reflect Plains influence [Steward, "Northern and Gosiute Shoshone," 282–86].

[303] Steward, "Northern and Gosiute Shoshone," 286.

[304] Liljeblad, "Oral Tradition: Content and Style of Verbal Arts," 653; see also Anne M. Smith, *Ute Tales* (Salt Lake City: University of Utah Press, 1992), 109–13, for several Ute stories about water babies and the dangers they posed.

[305] Liljeblad, "Oral Tradition," 653.

[306] Steward, "Northern and Gosiute Shoshone," 286.

[307] Ibid.

[308] Ibid.

[309] See Hultkrantz, "Mythology and Religious Concepts," and Liljeblad, "Oral Tradition," for more on this.

[310] Weixelman, 54.

[311] Ibid., 60.

[312] Steward, "Northern and Gosiute Shoshone," 282. See also brief discussion in Chapter 4 on the Sheepeaters.

[313] See the excellent discussion on this topic in Nabokov and Loendorf, 320–22.

[314] Beal, *Man in Yellowstone,* 91.

[315] Bartlett, 28.

[316] Haines, vol. 1, 248.

[317] Ibid.

[318] Bartlett, 28.

[319] Wingate, 140. At the end of the book Wingate offers descriptions of the flora and fauna of the Yellowstone region, details of the kinds of gear (especially firearms) one should have if venturing into the wilds of Yellowstone, distances between important natural features, and advice on how long to stay and the condition of the roads.

[320] Haines, vol. 2, 474.

[321] Moses Harris, *Report of the Superintendent of the Yellowstone National Park to the Secretary of the Interior, 1889* (Washington: Government Printing Office 1889), 13.

[322] Ibid., 14–15.

[323] Ibid., 16–19.

[324] Ibid., 15. See also Mark D. Spence, "First Wilderness: Indian Removal from Yellowstone National Park" (Paper presented at "People and Place: The Human Experience in Greater Yellowstone," Fourth Biennial Conference on the Greater Yellowstone Ecosystem, Mammoth, Wyoming, October 12–15, 1997).

[325] Harris, 16.

[326] B. Madsen, *Northern Shoshoni,* 242.

[327] *Report of the Commissioner of Indian Affairs, 1896,* 61.

[328] B. Madsen, *Northern Shoshoni,* 133, 134.

[329] B. Madsen, *The Bannock,* 253. See also Wright, *People of the High Country,* 156, for specifics on the role of the guides in this affair.

[330] *Report of the Commissioner of Indian Affairs,* "Disturbances in Jackson's Hole Country Wyoming," Ex. Document No. 5, 54th Congress 1st Session (1896), 62.

[331] Harris, 16.

[332] Capt. George S. Anderson, *Annual Report of the Superintendent of the Yellowstone National Park for the Year 1896* (Washington : Government Printing Office, 1896), 11.

[333] *Report to the Commissioner of Indian Affairs for 1896*, 79.

[334] B. Madsen, *Bannock of Idaho*, 257.

[335] *Report to the Commissioner of Indian Affairs, 1896*, 76.

[336] Accounts of this event are several. See, for example, B. Madsen, *Bannock of Idaho*, Chapter 10 ; Wright, *People of the High Country*, 156–57. The information presented here is taken from "Disturbances in 'Jackson Hole' Country Wyoming," 60–80.

[337] *Report to the Commissioner of Indian Affairs, 1896*, 68.

[338] B. Madsen, *Bannock of Idaho*, 260 ; *Report to the Commissioner of Indian Affairs, 1896*, 64.

[339] B. Madsen, *The Bannock*, 260.

[340] *Report to the Commissioner of Indian Affairs, 1896*, 64.

[341] B. Madsen, *The Bannock*, 261–62.

[342] These details are provided by Ben Senowin, a Bannock, who was one of the party assaulted. See *Report to the Commissioner of Indian Affairs, 1896*, 79.

[343] Ibid., 77.

[344] Ibid., 75.

[345] The complete report of the court findings can be found in *Report to the Commissioner of Indian Affairs*, Ex. Document No. 5, 54th Congress 2nd Session (1897), 60–66. Additional details of the Jackson Hole War of 1895 are presented in B. Madsen, *Bannock of Idaho*, 250–70 ; and B. Madsen, *Northern Shoshoni*, 137–38. A paraphrasing of an anonymous account is in Wright, *People of the High Country*, 156–57. The anonymous account referenced by Wright is "Anonymous, Indian Disturbances in 'Jackson Hole' Country, Wyoming, 1895," *Annals of Wyoming* 16 (1944) : 5–23.

[346] B. Madsen, *Northern Shoshoni*, 138.

[347] F. G. Irwin, Jr., "Reports of Fort Hall Agency, in Report of Agents in Idaho," *Annual Report to the Commissioner of Indian Affairs* (Washington : Government Printing Office, 1897).

[348] B. Madsen, *The Bannock*, 269.

[349] Dean H. Green, *History of Island Park* (Ashton : Island Park–Gateway Publishing Co., 1990), 23.

[350] Ed Eagle and Sam Eagle, *West Yellowstone's 70th Anniversary : 1908–1978* (West Yellowstone, Montana : The Eagle Company, 1978), 2–33.

[351] Ibid., 3–18.

[352] Albright, 91.

[353] Keller and Turek, Chapter 4.

[354] See ibid. for a complete treatment of this relationship and its evolution, and Alvin Runte *Trains of Discovery* (Niwot : Roberts Rinehart Publishers, 1994 and

figure 17) for illustrations of the calendars and excellent discussion of National Parks and the railroads.

[355] Keller and Turek, 22–23 and references therein.

[356] George Catlin, *Letters and Notes on the Manners, Customs, and Conditions of the North American Indians, vol. I* (1844; reprint, New York: Dover Publications, 1973), 261–62.

[357] See R. J. McGee and R. L. Warms, *Anthropological Theory: An Introductory History*, 2nd ed. (Mountain View: Mayfield Publishing Company, 1999), 5–10 for a discussion of this brand of evolutionary theory in anthropology.

[358] Keller and Turek, 19. According to Keller and Turek, Catlin saw Indians as a "curiosity" and "remnants of the land's ancient past."

[359] The relationship between American Indians and National Parks is a complex topic and beyond the scope of this work. Keller and Turek speak at length on this topic and I refer the interested reader to this text for excellent discussions.